KANDI GALLATY

The BIBLE *in a* YEAR

A GUIDED SCRIPTURE
READING JOURNEY
FOR WOMEN

LIFEWAY PRESS®
NASHVILLE, TENNESSEE

Published by Lifeway Press® • © 2022 Kandi Gallaty

ISBN: 978-1-0877-5041-5
Item: 005834118
Dewey decimal classification: 242.2
Subject headings: DEVOTIONAL LITERATURE / BIBLE—STUDY AND TEACHING / WOMEN

All Scripture quotations are taken from the Christian Standard Bible®, Copyright © 2017 by Holman Bible Publishers. Used by permission. Christian Standard Bible® and CSB® are federally registered trademarks of Holman Bible Publishers.

To order additional copies of this resource, write to Lifeway Resources Customer Service; One Lifeway Plaza; Nashville, TN 37234; order online at www.lifeway.com; fax 615.251.5933; phone toll free 800.458.2772; or email orderentry@lifeway.com.

Printed in the United States of America

Lifeway Women Publishing • Lifeway Resources •
One Lifeway Plaza • Nashville, TN 37234

EDITORIAL TEAM, LIFEWAY WOMEN BIBLE STUDIES

Becky Loyd
Director, Lifeway Women

Tina Boesch
Manager

Chelsea Waack
Production Leader

Laura Magness
Content Editor

Lindsey Bush
Production Editor

Lauren Ervin
Graphic Designer

CONTENTS

ABOUT THE AUTHOR

KANDI GALLATY has been investing in the lives of women for more than a decade. She believes that there are three major sources to draw from when investing in the lives of others: God's Word, God's work in one's life, and God's Spirit. She is passionate about cultivating a biblical worldview from the truths of Scripture and teaching women how to steward the life experiences and lessons God has allowed in their lives. Together Kandi and her husband, Robby, lead Replicate Ministries. Kandi loves being a pastor's wife and serving alongside her husband at Long Hollow Baptist Church. Kandi is the author of *Disciple Her: Using the Word, Work, & Wonder of God to Invest in Women* and *Foundations New Testament, A 260-Day Bible Reading Plan for Teen Girls*. Kandi and Robby are the proud and thankful parents of two boys, Rig and Ryder, and live outside of Nashville, Tennessee.

INTRODUCTION

For more than a decade now, I have been reading, studying, and creating resources to help women get into the Word until the Word gets into them. Now, more than ever, we need God's Word to speak louder than all of the voices surrounding us all day long—and that is exactly why I created this reading plan.

One of my greatest joys is helping others learn how to be intentional about putting themselves in an environment for growth. My prayer is that, through this reading plan, you will start to catch the same fire I have for disciplined, joy-filled spiritual growth, and that it would stir a passion inside of you for more: more of God, more of His Word, more of His power.

As you embark on this journey, I hope you will experience what is only the start of a lifelong pursuit of the living, breathing, active Word of God. As you begin to see Scripture for what it is, as you start applying its truth and getting to know its author, I hope this year-long commitment becomes a part of your life that lasts well beyond the next fifty-two weeks. I am thrilled for you as you enter this time of getting to know God, encounter Jesus, and deepen your relationship with the Holy Spirit.

The Spirit wants to speak to every believer, and I promise He wants to speak to you also. This resource will take the guesswork out of your daily reading and give you an opportunity to reflect on what you're hearing from God. Inside, you will find creative outlets, abiding truths, and nuggets of information that will make God's Word come alive and take root in your heart. It will teach you how to read and mine the text of Scripture for yourself so that regardless of when you are spending time in the Word, you know how to use it to create an environment to hear God speak.

Each element of this resource is meant to enhance your daily time with the Lord. I truly could not be more excited for you as you start *The Bible in a Year* reading plan. I prayed for you while I wrote this resource, and I'll be praying for you as I use it myself. May the Word of God dwell in you richly, and may you love God more passionately because of it.

Kandi Gallaty

Kandi Gallaty

HOW TO USE THIS STUDY

The Bible in a Year is a guided Scripture reading journey based on a Bible-reading plan my husband, Robby, and I developed, along with the help of our Replicate Ministries team. This reading plan, called the Foundational 260 (F260), is a 260-day reading plan that highlights the foundational passages of Scripture every disciple should know. **You'll find a checklist version of the full plan on pages 274–282.** As with any journey you set out on, it's helpful to know what lies ahead.

GETTING STARTED

The Bible in a Year is first and foremost a Bible-reading plan. Each week you'll be asked to read one or two chapters of Scripture a day for five days. (The two off days a week are built in so that you can catch up on days when you're unable to read.) I encourage you to begin each day in prayer, asking God to speak to you through His Word. After you pray, read that day's chapters designated at the top of the page. This plan also encourages you to keep a H.E.A.R.T. journal, memorize Bible verses, and dig deeper into the text and themes of your reading— regular disciplines that will help you digest more of the Word.

H.E.A.R.T. JOURNALING

The H.E.A.R.T. journal helps you read the Bible in a way that can change your life. No longer will you focus on checking off boxes on your daily reading schedule; instead, you'll be reading in order to understand and respond to God's Word. H.E.A.R.T. stands for Highlight, Explain, Apply, Respond, and Truth. The Spirit of God is speaking all the time; however, we often don't put ourselves in an environment in which we can hear Him. If you can commit to finding a consistent time to read Scripture and focus on what God has to say, then your heart and life will be changed.

Here's how it works. Say you're about to start 2 Timothy. Before reading the day's text, pause to ask sincerely that God speak to you. It may seem trite, but it's absolutely imperative that we seek God's guidance in order to understand His Word (see 1 Cor. 2:12-14). Every time we open our Bibles, we should pray the simple prayer David prayed:

> Open my eyes so that I may contemplate
> wondrous things from your instruction [Word].
>
> *PSALM 119:18*

As you read, one or two verses may speak to you. After reading the passage of Scripture, **highlight each verse that speaks to you by copying it under the letter H.** Record the following:

- The name of the book
- The passage of Scripture
- The chapter and verse numbers that especially speak to you
- A title to describe the passage

Next, **fill in the E section, for explain.** Here, you'll explain what the text means. By asking some simple questions, with the help of God's Spirit, you can understand the meaning of a passage or verse. Here are a few questions to keep in mind:

- Why was this text written?
- To whom was it originally written?
- How does this text fit with the verses before and after it?
- Why did the Holy Spirit include this passage in the book?
- What does the Holy Spirit intend to communicate through this text?

At this point you're beginning the process of discovering the specific, personal word God has for you from His Word. You're engaging with the text and wrestling with its meaning— reading the Bible the way it was meant to be read.

After writing a short summary of what you think the text means, **fill in the A section, for apply.** This application is the heart of the process. Everything you've done so far culminates under this heading. Again, answer a series of questions to uncover how these verses affect your life personally, questions like:

- What does this text teach me about God?
- What does this passage mean today?
- What would the application of this passage look like in my life?
- Does the text identify an action or attitude to avoid or embrace?
- Is there a promise to cling to or a truth to proclaim over my life?
- What is God saying to me?

Challenge yourself to write between two to five sentences about how the text applies to your life. These questions are important—they bring the words to life. The Bible is a living, breathing book, meant to be woven into our day-to-day lives. This section will show you the way. And don't feel limited by the space on the pages of this book. If you're short on space, you can always use a second journal or attach a piece of paper to that day's journal page in your book.

After the first three entries, **fill in the R section, for respond.** Your response to the passage may take on many forms. You might describe how you'll be different because of what you learned. You might write a prayer to God, or the name of a person to pray for or a friend who needs to hear the gospel.

Finally, write down a Truth. When you reflect on what you just read, what truth in the text sticks out to you? It can be a truth about God or about mankind. For example, if you are reading Genesis 1, a truth from that text is that God is Creator of everything. There are truths all throughout the Bible. Record them as you begin to see them. As you journey in your Christian life there will be many times you need to remind yourself of these truths. **You can see an example of a H.E.A.R.T. entry on page 271.**

Notice that most of the words in the H.E.A.R.T. formula are action words: highlight, explain, apply, and respond. God doesn't want us to sit back and wait for Him to drop truth into our laps. He wants us to actively pursue Him. Jesus said:

> Ask, and it will be given to you. Seek, and you will find. Knock, and the door will be opened to you.
>
> *MATTHEW 7:7*

Think of the miracle of the Bible. The Bible is composed of sixty-six different books, forty different authors, written more than fifteen hundred years ago across three different continents and in two languages. The Holy Spirit supernaturally led His people to write down the exact words of God. These words are divine, different from anything else that has ever been written. Not only have God's people brought these sixty-six books together but they have been preserved, an act almost as miraculous as its writing. Finally, God gave His people the technological knowledge to copy and transmit the Bible so that all people could have it. All because God has something to say to you.

MEMORIZING THE WORD

There are lots of ways to memorize Scripture, but my method is simple. All you need are a pack of index cards and a committed desire to memorize God's Word. It's easy. Write the verse reference on one side of the card and the text of the verse on the other. **Turn to page 272 to see a sample memory verse card.** You'll also find **free printables available for download at lifeway.com/bibleinayear.** Focus on memorizing five verses at a time and carry your pack of Scripture cards with you. Whenever you have a few minutes during the day, pull out your pack of Scripture cards and review them. Read the reference first, then the verse. Recite the verse over and over until you get a feel for the flow of the passage. When you think you've got it, turn over the card to the reference side to test your memory.

It's important to recite the reference when you start and when you finish so that you always know where a verse originates when you need it. This is crucial. When I was a new believer, sometimes I would quote Scripture while witnessing to someone, only to have the person ask me, "Where did you get that?" I could only answer, "Um . . . somewhere in the Bible." As you can imagine, that's not a convincing answer for a non-believer. By memorizing the references, you'll speak with authority and gain the respect of your listeners when you quote Scripture.

After you master five verses, take on five more. Review all the verses you've learned at least once a week. Soon you'll have a stack of index cards in your hand—and in your head. As your pack grows, you'll experience Scripture's powerful effects in your life.

DIGGING DEEPER

In addition to the daily readings and H.E.A.R.T. journaling, Days 2–4 of each week also offer you the chance to dig deeper into your Bible study for the days when you have the time. On the side of each page, you'll find a little something extra from one of these categories:

DID YOU KNOW?	Additional insights into the Scripture passage you read that day
THINK ABOUT IT	Thoughts to ponder or ways to pray
DAILY CHALLENGE	Activities and questions to help you learn more and apply what you've learned to your daily life
KEY WORD	Definitions that bring clarity or context to what you read
READ ON	A look at other passages of Scripture that expand on your reading

LEADING A GROUP THROUGH *THE BIBLE IN A YEAR?*

I'm so glad you've said yes to God's call to make disciples and chose *The Bible in a Year* to help you do so. Before your group year begins, make sure you have a copy of *The Bible in a Year Launch Kit,* which you can purchase at **lifeway.com/bibleinayear**. The Launch Kit includes:

- A video just for leaders with insight I've learned over years of leading year-long groups;
- Four videos for your group to watch during your first month together, so you have a better sense of what to expect; and
- A copy of my book *Disciple Her: Using the Word, Work, & Wonder of God to Invest in Women.*

And don't miss the helpful tools for you to use to promote your group in your church or community—such as a sample week, poster, and invitation card—at **lifeway.com/bibleinayear**.

Let's get started!

Guard your heart
above all else,
for it is the
source of life.

PROVERBS 4:23

DAY 1 | GENESIS 1-2

MEMORY VERSES: GENESIS 1:27; HEBREWS 11:7

The first two chapters of the Bible establish the biblical worldview all Christians should have regarding the natural world, human identity, and human relationships. These chapters affirm God as a sovereign, loving Creator, speaking the natural world into existence for His glory. He made humankind in His image, linking their identity to His own. He also made male and female as partners who complement one another and model the unity in diversity of the body of Christ.

HIGHLIGHT the verses that speak to you.

EXPLAIN what this passage means.

APPLY what God is saying in these verses to your life.

WEEK AT A GLANCE
I am so excited as we begin this journey together! We'll start "In the beginning . . ." with the creation of the world and the creation of man and woman. Sin entered the world quickly, yet we'll see that God's faithfulness never wavered. Because we're reading chronologically, we'll also begin the book of Job, which has much to teach us about what suffering looks like for the child of God.

RESPOND to what you've read.

TRUTH to remember and share.

DAY 2 | GENESIS 3-4

MEMORY VERSES: GENESIS 1:27; HEBREWS 11:7

DAILY CHALLENGE

List the consequences God relayed to the serpent, Adam, and Eve. Pay special attention to Genesis 3:15, the first glimpse of the good news of the gospel—God's saving grace through Jesus—that we see in Scripture.

In these two chapters we read how God's perfect creation was made imperfect through the cunning deceit of the serpent, or Satan, one of God's own creation who rebelled against Him. The serpent convinced Eve to doubt God's goodness, and in response she disobeyed God and convinced Adam to do the same. We know this event as the fall of man. With that single act of disobedience, sin entered the world. The negative impact of sin is felt in all of creation. Through Adam and Eve, sin became an inevitable part of human nature.

MEMORY VERSE

Pick one of the memory verse options for this week—Genesis 1:27; Hebrews 11:7—and write the verse. I suggest using the printable blank notecards available for free download at lifeway.com/bibleinayear!

H

E

A

R

T

DAY 3 | GENESIS 6-7

MEMORY VERSES: GENESIS 1:27; HEBREWS 11:7

It didn't take long for sin to wreak havoc on God's perfect creation. Notice how quickly the human race spiraled in its depravity. Humanity was created to worship and obey God, and because that no longer took place, God acted in judgment against the world's sin by sending a flood to wipe out the entire human race. In as much as God is just, though, these chapters also give evidence of His mercy through the fact that Noah and his family found favor in God's eyes. He subsequently spared their lives. All of Scripture affirms that these two aspects of God's character—His justice and mercy—remain in perfect harmony at all times.

DID YOU KNOW?
Don't miss all the examples of obedience found in the account of Noah:

- Noah obeyed;
- Nature obeyed;
- The animals obeyed;
- And all who obeyed were saved.

H

E

A

R

T

DAY 4 | GENESIS 8-9

MEMORY VERSES: GENESIS 1:27; HEBREWS 11:7

KEY WORD: WIND

In the Bible "wind" is often a visual depiction of the Spirit. The same Hebrew word for wind in Genesis 8:1 is used in Genesis 1:2 to describe the Spirit "hovering over the surface of the waters" and in Genesis 3:8 when we read, "The man and his wife heard the sound of the LORD God walking in the garden at the time of the evening breeze."

MEMORY VERSE

Continue practicing the memory verse you chose. Write out as much of it as you can from memory, and then check to see how you did.

Genesis 8-9 records the aftermath of the flood. Noah and his family faithfully obeyed God, and God faithfully protected them from His judgment. We are reminded of God's love for humans—those He created in His own image. God used Noah's family to once again populate the earth with His people. In what is known as the Noahic covenant, God promised to never again destroy the earth and its inhabitants with a flood, a promise He has kept to this day. God sealed this promise with a rainbow, a sign that God keeps His promises.

H

E

A

R

T

DAY 5 | JOB 1–2

MEMORY VERSES: GENESIS 1:27; HEBREWS 11:7

The book of Job, which is set during the patriarchal period making it a contemporary to early Genesis accounts, addresses the issue of God's allowance of suffering in the lives of His people. The early chapters of Genesis describe sin's entrance into and corruption of the world. We also realize that human suffering is an inevitable consequence of sin. Job 1–2 reminds us that even the most faithful of God's people are not exempt from suffering and sin. However, these chapters also remind us that because God is sovereign, everything—even suffering—has a purpose that ultimately leads to His glory and fulfillment of His plans. The purpose of Job's suffering was that the world would see the life-transforming power of genuine faith in God.

H

E

A

R

T

WEEK IN REVIEW
Spend some time reflecting on what you have learned this week. Record a truth from each day that you want to remember, or go back and highlight portions of your journal.

DAY 1:

DAY 2:

DAY 3:

DAY 4:

DAY 5:

DAY 6 | JOB 38-39

MEMORY VERSES: HEBREWS 11:6; HEBREWS 11:8-10

Last week's reading ended with Job 1–2, which describes the suffering God allowed Job to endure as a way for God to be glorified. In chapters 3–37 Job wrestled with his despair both privately and in the company of friends. In Job 38 God finally speaks. His words to Job were a reminder that the person Job questioned was the Almighty Creator and Sustainer of the universe. Job's story reveals that God is in control, His ways are best, and everything exists to bring glory to His name.

H

E

A

R

T

WEEK AT A GLANCE
Congratulations on finishing your first week of reading through the Bible in a year! This week we'll pick back up in Job, where we'll read about God's response to Job's suffering. Then we'll find ourselves back in Genesis reading about the call of Abraham.

DAY 7 | JOB 40-42

MEMORY VERSES: HEBREWS 11:6; HEBREWS 11:8-10

After being reminded of the holiness and power of God, Job could do nothing but confess his sins, turn back to God, and renew his trust in the Lord. He said, "I reject my words and am sorry for them; I am dust and ashes" (Job 42:6). In the face of God's holiness, we are reminded that apart from Him, we are nothing but dust from the ground, and to dust we "will return" (Gen. 3:19). Yet through Job's experience we are reminded that God gives physical life through His very breath, and He gives spiritual life through the death and resurrection of His Son. These are gifts we do not deserve, and they motivate us to mimic Job's life of confession and repentance, continually stripping away the things that keep us from trusting God in all things.

THINK ABOUT IT
A full understanding of God's reasons for the events in your life is not a prerequisite for faithfulness. We don't know if Job was ever told the reason why he suffered so horribly. However, we are told in Ezekiel (twice!) that Job was righteous (Ezek. 14:14,20).

MEMORY VERSE
Pick one of the memory verse options for this week—Hebrews 11:6; Hebrews 11:8-10—and write the verse.

H

E

A

R

T

DAY 8 | GENESIS 11-12

MEMORY VERSES: HEBREWS 11:6; HEBREWS 11:8-10

DAILY CHALLENGE

Consider areas of your life where you may be building a name for yourself—work, school, family, social media, and so on—and list any that come to mind. Ask yourself if you are pointing others toward God and His glory or toward you and your glory. Spend some time in prayer, confessing that to Him and asking for forgiveness. Read Ephesians 2:1-10 for a loving reminder that we have no one to boast in but God.

Through Noah's family the earth was repopulated after the flood, and Genesis 11 states that people shared a common language and a common goal—making a name for themselves. As had happened twice before in Genesis 3–10, people created by God to glorify Him put their efforts toward glorifying themselves instead. And yet again humanity's sin brought God's judgment. Yet despite the people's continued sinfulness, we see God's covenant love for humanity through the promise He made with Abram in Genesis 12—a promise to bless all the people of the earth through Himself. This promise ultimately found its fulfillment in Jesus Christ, who descended from the genealogical line of Abram, and through whom all people have access to the grace and redemption of God.

H

E

A

R

T

DAY 9 | GENESIS 15

MEMORY VERSES: HEBREWS 11:6; HEBREWS 11:8-10

God promised to make Abram into a great nation, but Abram and his wife were childless. While Abram waited for God to fulfill His promise, years went by, and no children came. Then God spoke to Abram again, this time making an even more specific promise that Abram would have a son, which would then lead to offspring as numerous as the stars. Genesis 15:6 says that despite the prolonged years of barrenness, Abram believed God, and that belief made him righteous, or put him in a right relationship with God. Likewise, when we believe in the gospel—the death and resurrection of Jesus for our salvation—God considers us righteous too.

DID YOU KNOW?

- Abraham (then Abram) was called from Ur when he was 75.
- Abraham fathered Ishmael with Hagar when he was 85 or 86.
- Abraham fathered Isaac with Sarah when he was 100.
- Sarah died when Abraham was 137.
- Abraham died when he was 175.[1]

MEMORY VERSE

Continue practicing the memory verse you chose. Write out as much of it as you can from memory, and then check to see how you did.

H

E

A

R

T

MEMORY VERSES: HEBREWS 11:6; HEBREWS 11:8-10

WEEK IN REVIEW

Spend some time reflecting on what you have learned this week. Record a truth from each day that you want to remember, or go back and highlight portions of your journal.

In Genesis 16 the focus shifts from Abram to his wife, Sarai. All they knew of God's promise was that they would have an heir, so Sarai took the initiative to provide that heir herself by using Hagar, her servant, as a surrogate mother. Sarai's actions revealed a lack of trust in God's ability to provide. God alone was the engineer of Abram and Sarai's destiny, and their attempts to go about it alone paled in comparison to the grandeur of God's plan. Once more in Genesis 17 God reminded Abram that He would be the one to bless them, He would give them the promised son, Isaac, He would make their descendants as numerous as the stars, and He would receive all of the glory. God's faithfulness and ability to do what He says overcomes all of our flaws and uncertainties.

DAY 1:

DAY 2:

H

DAY 3:

E

DAY 4:

A

DAY 5:

R

T

DAY 11 | GENESIS 18–19

MEMORY VERSES: ROMANS 4:20-22; HEBREWS 11:17-19

In Genesis 18 three visitors appeared to Abraham and reaffirmed God's promise to give Abraham and Sarah a son. Just before the visitors left, Abraham learned that God was about to judge the cities of Sodom and Gomorrah for their sins. Abraham questioned God's mercy and justice, and when God stated that He would spare the city for ten righteous people, Abraham understood the breadth and depth of God's love and mercy (18:22-33). Unfortunately, God already knew that ten righteous people would not be found in the city, and chapter 19 records the destruction that came to them as a result. Sin is a violation of the very character of God, and because He is just, He must take action against it. Thankfully, the finality of God's action took place at the cross, when Jesus bore God's wrath for our sin once and for all.

H

E

A

R

T

> **WEEK AT A GLANCE**
> We're in for a week of ups and downs, which I'm so thankful for in Scripture, aren't you? We'll read about God reaffirming His promise to Abraham, the destruction of Sodom and Gomorrah, Isaac's birth, and how Abraham was tested. We'll end the week with a marriage and the birth of twins. That's a lot of ground to cover, so let's get going!

MEMORY VERSES: ROMANS 4:20-22; HEBREWS 11:17-19

THINK ABOUT IT

God is and will always be our greatest advocate, and He should be the One in whom we place our ultimate trust. God may not remove the difficulties we face, but He will reveal Himself through them. The way God intervened in Sarah's and Hagar's lives reminds us that He always hears us and sees us.

MEMORY VERSE

Pick one of the memory verse options for this week—Romans 4:20-22; Hebrews 11:17-19—and write the verse.

Despite God's continued faithfulness, Abraham still had a hard time learning to trust God in all things. Afraid for his life, Abraham lied about Sarah's identity and put the entire kingdom in jeopardy. Even so, God's faithfulness to His covenant promises shone through as He protected Abraham in spite of his sin. Next, as God had promised, Sarah became pregnant by Abraham and delivered a son at the exact time God had specified. These two chapters speak to God's promise-keeping nature. Thankfully, as Abraham's life demonstrates, God is faithful to His promises no matter how many times His children sin and stumble. God's love outweighs even our biggest weaknesses.

H

E

A

R

T

DAY 13 | GENESIS 22

MEMORY VERSES: ROMANS 4:20-22; HEBREWS 11:17-19

The story of Abraham's testing in Genesis 22 is one of the most famous stories about his life. After waiting years for God to fulfill His promise of a son, imagine Abraham's shock when God asked him to sacrifice his only son to Him. Immediately Abraham set off to obey God in faith, but as Abraham prepared to sacrifice his son, God stopped him and provided a sacrificial ram in Isaac's place. Abraham's willingness to sacrifice his son in obedience to God reminds us how God has done the same for us. God gave His only Son, Jesus, to die for us as a sacrifice for our sins. If God is willing to sacrifice the One He loves most, why would we not offer everything, even our lives, as living sacrifices back to Him (Rom. 12:1-2)?

DAILY CHALLENGE

Read and compare Genesis 22:18 and Matthew 28:19-20. Are you living in obedience to the command God has given you as a follower of Jesus? Who will be blessed because you have obeyed?

H

E

A

R

T

DAY 14 | GENESIS 24

MEMORY VERSES: ROMANS 4:20-22; HEBREWS 11:17-19

DID YOU KNOW?

Isaac is a type of Christ, meaning parts of his story foreshadow Jesus's person and/ or His work. The first time we see Isaac after the sacrifice on Mount Moriah (Gen. 22) is when he claimed his bride in Genesis 24. The first time we will see Jesus after His sacrificial death and resurrection is when He comes to claim His bride!

MEMORY VERSE

Continue practicing the memory verse you chose. Write out as much of it as you can from memory, and then check to see how you did.

Time and again throughout Abraham's story, we see God acting faithfully according to the promises He made Abraham. One of those promises was that Abraham's offspring would inherit the land of Canaan, which became known as the promised land (Gen. 12:7). Realizing he was getting old, Abraham planned for Isaac's future. He summoned a servant and sent him to find a wife for Isaac. Abraham was confident that God's hand would guide them, so his servant also trusted that it would happen, and it did. Through a series of events, God revealed that Rebekah was to be Isaac's future wife. This part of Abraham's story reminds us that our all-knowing, all-powerful God is continually at work in and through us to accomplish His good purposes.

H

E

A

R

T

DAY 15 | GENESIS 25:19-34; 26

MEMORY VERSES: ROMANS 4:20-22; HEBREWS 11:17-19

Isaac married Rebekah, and like Sarah, Rebekah had difficulty conceiving children. But after Isaac prayed to God, she conceived twin boys—Esau and Jacob. Early on, animosity ran deep between these two brothers. One day, when Esau came home exhausted from an unsuccessful hunt, Jacob sold him a bowl of soup in exchange for Esau's birthright, the first recorded instance of what would become a lifelong sibling rivalry rooted in jealousy and pride. These were Isaac's sons, so they too were children of the promise—God's covenant with Abraham—and like the covenant He had with Abraham, God promised to bless Isaac and his offspring. By pointing out many of Isaac's, Jacob's, and Esau's sins, the writer of Genesis (Moses) reminds us again that God's faithfulness to and love of His people has nothing to do with them and has everything to do with Him.

H

E

A

R

T

WEEK IN REVIEW
Spend some time reflecting on what you have learned this week. Record a truth from each day that you want to remember, or go back and highlight portions of your journal.

DAY 1:

DAY 2:

DAY 3:

DAY 4:

DAY 5:

DAY 16 | GENESIS 27-28

MEMORY VERSES: 2 CORINTHIANS 10:12; 1 JOHN 3:18

When Isaac was old and blind, Jacob deceived him into giving him the family blessing instead of Esau, the older son to whom it rightfully belonged. Esau responded to this deception with anger and murderous thoughts, so Jacob had no choice but to escape and seek refuge with more extended family, at which time he also sought out a wife. As God had done with Isaac and Abraham, He spoke to Jacob at the start of his journey and reiterated His covenant promises for their family. With that event, Jacob's life took a turn away from the deception and selfishness of his youth toward his future as a faithful patriarch who would lead his family to trust in the Lord. God's promise to Jacob—"Look, I am with you and will watch over you wherever you go" (Gen. 28:15)—remains His life-changing promise to us today through the once-for-all sacrifice of Jesus.

H

E

A

R

T

WEEK AT A GLANCE
Today starts Week 4, and I'm so proud of you! You're one month into reading God's Word regularly and recording what He's speaking to your heart. One of the beauties of journaling in response to your Bible reading each day is that your words can be passed on to someone else. You're leaving a legacy of faithfulness and a testimony of God's goodness. Praise God!

DAY 17 | GENESIS 29–30:24

MEMORY VERSES: 2 CORINTHIANS 10:12; 1 JOHN 3:18

The beginning of Jacob's own family and the birth of several of his children is documented in the next chapters of Genesis. Deception and envy are two key issues that permeated this family's relationships. Jacob deceived his father and his brother, then found himself on the receiving end of deception from Laban, who promised Jacob one daughter in marriage but tricked him into marrying another. Eventually, Jacob married both Leah and Rachel, and their ability and inability (respectively) to have children became the source of yet more jealousy and envy. As is God's providential nature, from these corrupted relationships came twelve sons who eventually became the heads of the twelve tribes of Israel. Even better, one of those tribes—the tribe of Judah—would eventually bring forth the Messiah, God's promised deliverer of His people, Jesus Christ our Redeemer.

H

E

A

R

T

DAILY CHALLENGE

Comparison will never give you confidence or fulfill your God-given calling. In fact, it's a way the enemy keeps us from being the women God has created us to be. List below or in a separate notebook some of your talents, gifts, and passions. You are a uniquely-gifted and beautiful woman, and there is no need to ever compare yourself to anyone else.

MEMORY VERSE

Pick one of the memory verse options for this week—
2 Corinthians 10:12;
1 John 3:18—and write the verse.

DAY 18 | GENESIS 31–32

MEMORY VERSES: 2 CORINTHIANS 10:12; 1 JOHN 3:18

KEY WORD: ISRAEL

Jacob's new name, Israel, refers to "the concept of wrestling, clinging firmly to God, and overcoming . . . Israel is to be understood as Jacob's covenant name. The name spoke of his being bound with a bond of life and love to God."[2]

READ ON

Hosea 12:2-6

As a result of God's grace and power in Jacob's life, he experienced great prosperity during these years, which became yet another source of jealousy among his extended family. Again God appeared to Jacob in a dream, this time urging Jacob to take his family and return home to Canaan. When Jacob and his family left, Laban pursued them, but God again proved faithful to protect and deliver Jacob from harm. Unfortunately, home did not hold the promise of peace for Jacob either because he was returning to his brother Esau, who in their last encounter threatened to kill Jacob. Genesis 32 highlights the anxiety Jacob felt about the crisis, which led to an unexpected encounter with God. From Jacob's wrestling match with God, we are reminded that God will go to great lengths in order to teach us dependency on Him and the sufficiency of His grace.

H

E

A

R

T

DAY 19 | GENESIS 33; 35

MEMORY VERSES: 2 CORINTHIANS 10:12; 1 JOHN 3:18

The reunion of Jacob and Esau is one of the greatest pictures of reconciliation in Scripture (Gen. 33). Enough time and life experience had passed between the two brothers that the grudges of their youth were forgotten, and Jacob noted, "I have seen your face, and it is like seeing God's face" (Gen. 33:10). Only the Lord's work in their lives could bring about such change. Through that reunion and some other horrific events described in Genesis 34, Jacob realized that he and his family needed to renew their commitment to the Lord. Genesis 35 describes that renewal of their commitment to God and God's covenant promises to them. Scripture is filled with many promises from God that still apply to His children today. Regularly strengthening our commitment to God and claiming His promises is a vital part of the life of a Christ follower.

DAILY CHALLENGE

What are some of God's promises to you that you can recall from Scripture? Read Psalm 16:11; Romans 8:1; Philippians 1:6; and 1 John 1:9 for just a sampling of the promises that are yours in Christ.

H

E

A

R

T

MEMORY VERSE

Continue practicing the memory verse you chose. Write out as much of it as you can from memory, and then check to see how you did.

DAY 20 | GENESIS 37

MEMORY VERSES: 2 CORINTHIANS 10:12; 1 JOHN 3:18

WEEK IN REVIEW
Spend some time reflecting on what you have learned this week. Record a truth from each day that you want to remember, or go back and highlight portions of your journal.

DAY 1:

DAY 2:

DAY 3:

DAY 4:

DAY 5:

With Genesis 37 the story of God's chosen people shifts from Jacob to his son Joseph, who is the main character throughout the rest of Genesis. Rachel struggled to have children, and Joseph was the first child she was able to bear. Because Rachel was Jacob's favorite wife, Joseph became Jacob's favorite son, which meant blessings from his father and ridicule from his brothers. In what has become one of the most well-known accounts in the Old Testament, Joseph was sold into slavery by his brothers, who then lied to their father by telling him Joseph was dead. This set in motion a series of trials Joseph would face over many years, but early on in his story, we see evidence that God was orchestrating the events of Joseph's life. God gave Joseph the power to interpret dreams, a divine gift that would determine the course his life would take to protect God's covenant people.

H

E

A

R

T

DAY 21 | GENESIS 39–40

MEMORY VERSES: ROMANS 8:28-30; EPHESIANS 3:20-21

Joseph's brothers sold him as a slave to the Midianites, who took Joseph to Egypt where he was sold to Potiphar, an officer of Pharaoh. Potiphar increasingly respected Joseph, and over time Joseph's authority in Potiphar's house increased. His loyalty to Potiphar resulted in an attempted seduction by his master's wife. The short-term result was Joseph's undeserved imprisonment. Yet in spite of this and other setbacks, Joseph knew God was with him, and the opportunity to put his God-given gift of dream interpretation to work further supported God's active presence in Joseph's life.

H

E

A

R

T

WEEK AT A GLANCE
Week 5 is all about God's work through the life of Joseph. We can learn so much through his story, including the many ways Joseph's story points us forward to Jesus.

DAY 22 | GENESIS 41

MEMORY VERSES: ROMANS 8:28-30; EPHESIANS 3:20-21

THINK ABOUT IT

The names Joseph chose for his sons reveal that God made Joseph forget all his hardship and made him fruitful in the land of his affliction (Gen. 41:51-52). What fruit in your life has been born from affliction and adversity? Pray to the Lord, thanking Him for the fruit in your life that has come from pain and difficulty.

In Genesis 41 God's sovereignty is on display through Joseph's story in several key ways. God prepared Joseph to interpret Pharaoh's dream and positioned him at the appropriate time to do so. God put plans in place that enabled the Egyptians and others to survive the famine. God orchestrated Joseph's rise in power. Despite the actions of people like Joseph's brothers and Potiphar's wife, God put Joseph in a position where he would be able to protect and provide for God's covenant people.

MEMORY VERSE

Pick one of the memory verse options for this week— Romans 8:28-30; Ephesians 3:20-21— and write the verse.

H

E

A

R

T

DAY 23 | GENESIS 42-43

MEMORY VERSES: ROMANS 8:28-30; EPHESIANS 3:20-21

The famine Joseph predicted from Pharaoh's dreams came to be, and its impact reached beyond Egypt even to Canaan, Joseph's homeland. In another demonstration of God's providence, Joseph's rise in power combined with the horrific effects of the famine in Canaan brought Joseph and his brothers together. Joseph controlled the distribution of grain for the region, and Jacob sent his sons to Egypt to buy some of that grain. Joseph's brothers did not recognize him, so he put an intricate plan for reunion in place. At the heart of Joseph's plan was a desire to see his father again and be reconciled to his brothers.

DAILY CHALLENGE
Many parts of Joseph's story point the reader forward to the story of Jesus, the Son of God and ultimate Savior of God's people. If you're familiar with Jesus and the Gospels, then make a list of how many parallels you can find between Joseph and Jesus. (If you're not familiar, stay tuned!) I will list a few below to get you started.

- Joseph was betrayed and sold into slavery; Jesus was betrayed, and His garments were sold.
- Joseph was stripped and mocked; Jesus was stripped and mocked.
-

H

E

A

R

T

DAY 24 | GENESIS 44-45

MEMORY VERSES: ROMANS 8:28-30; EPHESIANS 3:20-21

DAILY CHALLENGE

Is there someone you need to forgive in your life? Pray and ask the Lord how to go about forgiving this person. If you feel led to write a letter or an email, or grab lunch or coffee, be obedient to follow through. Forgiveness sets you free from continuing to carry the hurt, burden, and bitterness in your life.

Joseph's reunion with his brothers brought to light the maturity and compassion that had developed in them since their last meeting. When Joseph was sold into slavery, Judah orchestrated the events (Gen. 37). But when Benjamin was threatened with slavery, Judah offered his own life as a sacrifice in Benjamin's place because he knew the pain that losing Benjamin would cause to his father (Gen. 44). With this, Joseph knew his brothers had changed, and he could hide his identity no longer. The forgiveness and compassion Joseph showed to his brothers is a picture of the forgiveness and compassion God has shown us in Christ. Even though we have sinned against God, He loves us and made the ultimate sacrifice to draw us back to Himself.

MEMORY VERSE

Continue practicing the memory verse you chose. Write out as much of it as you can from memory, and then check to see how you did.

H

E

A

R

T

DAY 25 | GENESIS 46–47

MEMORY VERSES: ROMANS 8:28-30; EPHESIANS 3:20-21

The same famine that brought Joseph to power also brought his family to Egypt (Gen. 47:4). By moving the family to Egypt, Jacob (whom God renamed Israel) was reunited with his long lost son. Through Joseph's faithfulness to God and loyalty to Pharaoh, he was able to make a way for his family to settle in the land and escape the worst effects of the famine. Beyond that, Joseph also managed to keep Pharaoh prosperous and keep people fed during a tragic time in Egypt's history. Yet again God used an international disaster and the faithfulness of one person to advance His purposes for His covenant people.

H

E

A

R

T

WEEK IN REVIEW
Spend some time reflecting on what you have learned this week. Record a truth from each day that you want to remember, or go back and highlight portions of your journal.

DAY 1:

DAY 2:

DAY 3:

DAY 4:

DAY 5:

DAY 26 | GENESIS 48-49

MEMORY VERSES: GENESIS 50:20; HEBREWS 11:24-26

Joseph's story paints one big picture of God's faithfulness to His children and His promises. In these chapters, we see several examples of God's work through the lives of Jacob's family. Genesis 48 describes how Jacob adopted Manasseh and Ephraim, Joseph's Egyptian sons, into their family, which was the covenant family of God. When Jacob took them as his own sons (Gen. 48:5), he guaranteed that Joseph and his descendants would be a part of God's covenant community in the generations to come. Jesus's crucifixion and resurrection accomplished a similar purpose. Through the death and resurrection of Jesus, anyone who believes in Jesus becomes an adopted child of God and heir to all His promises (Rom. 8:12-17).

H

E

WEEK AT A GLANCE
Our readings this week will transition us from Joseph's leadership to Moses's. The Israelites multiplied and prospered in Egypt, but they became slaves over the years since Joseph's death. So God set in motion a great deliverance of His people. Let's dive in!

A

R

T

DAY 27 | GENESIS 50–EXODUS 1

MEMORY VERSES: GENESIS 50:20; HEBREWS 11:24-26

Fearing for their lives after Jacob's death, Joseph's brothers sought forgiveness and offered to be his slaves. Joseph then revealed his understanding that everything that had happened to him was part of God's larger plan (Gen. 50:20). In spite of all the hardships Joseph had suffered, God had positioned him perfectly to do the most good for the greatest number of people. Genesis 50:20 is one of the Bible's clearest affirmations of God's sovereignty—the fact that all things are under God's control and nothing happens apart from His plan and purpose. However, it wasn't long before that belief and the faithfulness of God's people was put to the test, as Exodus 1 describes. After Joseph died, the Israelites in Egypt were forced into slavery, and Pharaoh demanded all newborn baby boys be killed in order to keep the Israelite population from growing. Once again the stage was set for God to act on behalf of His people in order to bring glory to His name.

THINK ABOUT IT

Sin and suffering under the umbrella of God's sovereignty led to survival and salvation for an entire nation. What suffering in your life may God be intending for good? What does faithfulness look like for you in that situation?

MEMORY VERSE

Pick one of the memory verse options for this week—Genesis 50:20; Hebrews 11:24-26—and write the verse.

H

E

A

R

T

DAY 28 | EXODUS 2-3

MEMORY VERSES: GENESIS 50:20; HEBREWS 11:24-26

KEY WORD: BASKET

Exodus 2:3 says that Moses was placed in a basket in the river. The same Hebrew word for basket, *teba*, is also used for the ark that Noah built. Draw a picture of what you imagine Moses's basket/mini ark looked like. Draw a picture of what you imagine Noah's ark looked like. Both arks are pictures of God's salvation and deliverance of His people.

Throughout the Bible God calls individual people to play key roles in His redemptive plan, such as Noah, Abraham, Joseph, and Moses. God protected Moses during his birth because of the plans He had for Moses, and Moses grew up as an Egyptian prince. However, Moses's murderous action against an Egyptian slave forced him out of the land and into a new life in Midian, where he married and became a shepherd. It was there that Moses's well-known burning-bush encounter with God took place. When the Egyptian king died, the Israelites cried out to God for deliverance. He heard them and acted to save them. Using a burning bush to attract Moses's attention, God called him to lead the Israelites out of slavery. At that time, God also revealed to Moses His name—Yahweh, "I AM WHO I AM" (Ex. 3:14). One of the great truths about God is that He does not change, a fact tied up in His very identity and name. This helps us know that just as God was faithful in the lives of His Old Testament servants, He continues to prove Himself faithful to us today.

H

E

A

R

T

38 WEEK 6 | DAY 28 | EXODUS 2-3

DAY 29 | EXODUS 4-5

MEMORY VERSES: GENESIS 50:20; HEBREWS 11:24-26

God had big plans for Moses, but Moses was not convinced God picked the right man for the job. Moses voiced hesitation at what God asked of him, so God gave him three signs and promised to send his brother Aaron to assist him. Each of the signs—turning the staff into a snake, turning Moses's hand leprous, and turning water into blood—revealed God's power over the created world, which reminded Moses and all the Israelites that God also had the power to set them free. Convinced that he should obey God, Moses met up with Aaron, and the two assembled the Israelites and showed them God's signs. As a result, the people worshiped God, thanking Him for hearing their prayers (4:18-31). However, they had a long road to freedom. Chapter 5 describes Moses's and Aaron's first audience with Pharaoh, who responded to their request for freedom with a denial of God's existence and heavier oppression of the Israelites.

DID YOU KNOW?

Moses's life can be divided out into three sets of forty years:

- Egypt: 0–40 years old – Pharaoh's house
- Midian: 41–80 years old – shepherd
- Sinai/wilderness: 81–120 years old – deliverer[3]

MEMORY VERSE

Continue practicing the memory verse you chose. Write out as much of it as you can from memory, and then check to see how you did.

H

E

A

R

T

DAY 30 | EXODUS 6-7

MEMORY VERSES: GENESIS 50:20; HEBREWS 11:24-26

WEEK IN REVIEW

Spend some time reflecting on what you have learned this week. Record a truth from each day that you want to remember, or go back and highlight portions of your journal.

DAY 1:

DAY 2:

DAY 3:

DAY 4:

DAY 5:

When God called Moses, the plan was to use Moses to set the Israelites free. Yet in the eyes of the Israelites, that plan seemed to backfire. When Moses complained to God, God reminded Moses of His connection to Abraham, Isaac, and Jacob and reaffirmed His covenant with them. He promised to deliver the Israelites and to bring them to a new land, the promised land. God revealed that prolonging the Israelites' suffering had a purpose, just like the sufferings of Joseph and Job. Since Pharaoh would not let the Israelites go, God would bring His people out by His power. Through His wondrous acts the Egyptians would see the glory of God. Pharaoh's continued refusal to free God's people brought about the ten plagues, the first of which was the plague of blood. One must not miss the great truth about God tucked away in Exodus 6. In God's reassurance to Moses, He described the process of revelation and redemption by which all people are saved: "I will bring you out . . . I will redeem you . . . I will take you as my people, and I will be your God" (Ex. 6:6-7). Here again the cross of Christ was foreshadowed.

H

E

A

R

T

DAY 31 | EXODUS 8–9

MEMORY VERSES: JOHN 1:29; HEBREWS 9:22

Because Pharaoh refused to listen to Moses and free the Israelites from slavery, God unleashed a series of ten plagues on the nation, several of which are described in Exodus 8–9. The water in the Nile River turned to blood. Then frogs, gnats, and flies overran the land. One plague caused the death of livestock. Another brought boils, while another was a plague of deadly hail. As with everything God does, the goal of the plagues was that Pharaoh and the Egyptians would see His glory on display. Moses announced each plague, and each arrived and departed exactly as he stated. These announcements served as warnings to Pharaoh, and they gave him the opportunity to act. They also gave a testimony to God's grace. His plagues weren't set in stone, and had Pharaoh acknowledged God and freed His people, God would have extended grace to Pharaoh and the nation. However, Pharaoh would not relent. The plagues punished Egypt, showed the powerlessness of their gods, and demonstrated God's glory.

H

E

A

R

T

WEEK AT A GLANCE
Buckle up this week, friends! Our journey through the Bible will cover the main events of the exodus, from the plagues God sent to Egypt when Pharaoh refused to let Israel go, to God's miraculous deliverance of the Israelites from the Egyptians with the crossing of the Red Sea. This week finishes with God providing bread from heaven and water from a rock. The many miracles we'll reflect on this week remind us that nothing is impossible with God.

DAY 32 | EXODUS 10–11

MEMORY VERSES: JOHN 1:29; HEBREWS 9:22

READ ON

Read Psalm 105, a reflection on God's faithfulness to His people during this time in their history.

MEMORY VERSE

Pick one of the memory verse options for this week—John 1:29; Hebrews 9:22—and write the verse.

Exodus 10–11 describe the final three plagues—a swarm of locusts, darkness that descended over all of Egypt, and the plague on the firstborn. As with the previous plagues, Pharaoh initially repented but changed his mind after God withdrew the plague from the land. However, God told Moses that the final plague would be the last, and after that the people would be free. Again, the goal of the plagues was that everyone, the Israelites and the Egyptians, would recognize the power and glory of God. That's why He went into such detail with Moses's instructions in the first place. God left no room for justifiable doubt in people's minds as to who was in control. Exodus 11:5-7 reveals God's plan to protect the firstborn sons of the Israelites, further evidence that He would protect His people and continue to uphold His covenant with Abraham.

H

E

A

R

T

DAY 33 | EXODUS 12

MEMORY VERSES: JOHN 1:29; HEBREWS 9:22

On the night of the plague on the firstborn, God established Passover—a Jewish holiday that commemorates God's deliverance of the Israelites from Egypt. Passover got its name from the animal blood smeared on the door posts, which marked the Israelites apart from the Egyptians and served as a sign for God's angelic death to pass over the house without killing the firstborn. Once the plague came down on the people, Pharaoh summoned Moses and ordered the Israelites to leave. With that the Israelites began their exodus journey. Centuries later, Jesus Christ became the ultimate Passover Lamb when God sent Him to be the sacrifice to save people from the bondage of their sins once and for all. In Jesus all of the ritual aspects of the Passover described in Exodus 12 find their fulfillment.

DAILY CHALLENGE

If you are a new creation in Christ, then the Lord has set you free from slavery to sin and self. List some of the things God has freed you from, and write a prayer thanking Him for your freedom. There is power in remembering the mighty work God has done in your life.

H

E

A

R

T

DAY 34 | EXODUS 13:17–14

MEMORY VERSES: JOHN 1:29; HEBREWS 9:22

THINK ABOUT IT

A verse God has used to speak to me many times is Exodus 14:14, which says, "The LORD will fight for you, and you must be quiet." Sometimes God calls us to stand firm and be silent. He's more than capable of fighting for us in any situation. Write a prayer to God for a situation where you need Him to fight for you. Maybe God is calling you to say nothing, to be silent. Lay that before Him now and trust Him.

God's presence accompanied the Israelites from the very beginning of their exodus journey, as symbolized by the pillars of cloud and fire that led them on their way. The Israelites had not been out of Egypt long, though, when their fate seemed to take a turn for the worse. Once again God hardened Pharaoh's heart, and Pharaoh gathered an army to track down the Israelites. Exodus 14 makes it clear that this was all a part of God's plan. Moses encouraged the people to trust God, and this encounter culminated in the most famous event in the exodus—the parting of the Red Sea. Moses stretched his hand over the sea, God divided the waters, and the Israelites crossed on dry ground. When the Egyptians pursued the Israelites onto the dry sea floor, God brought the waters back together, drowning Pharaoh's army. With that single act, God acted in final judgment against Pharaoh, and the Israelites feared God and believed in Him (14:31).

H

E

MEMORY VERSE

Continue practicing the memory verse you chose. Write out as much of it as you can from memory, and then check to see how you did.

A

R

T

DAY 35 | EXODUS 16–17

MEMORY VERSES: JOHN 1:29; HEBREWS 9:22

The Israelites were free from slavery, but they were not free from hardship, a fact that God used to test their dependence on and obedience to Him. With food difficult to find in the wilderness, the Israelites remembered the days of Egyptian slavery when they at least had enough to eat. The people complained to Moses, and God responded by sending quail and manna—daily provisions of food to keep them satiated on their journey. God met the people's need for food (and then again for water in chapter 17), again revealing His care and provisions for His people. By sending the food daily, God forced the people to remain dependent on Him, something they struggled to do despite all the ways He had already provided for them. This struggle with trust would be the defining characteristic of the Israelites' forty years in the desert, and it is a good reminder for us when our trust in God wavers or we forget how faithful He truly is. Just as God provided water and food to sustain the Israelites, He has given us Jesus to forever quench the hunger and thirst of our souls (John 4).

H

E

A

R

T

WEEK IN REVIEW
Spend some time reflecting on what you have learned this week. Record a truth from each day that you want to remember, or go back and highlight portions of your journal.

DAY 1:

DAY 2:

DAY 3:

DAY 4:

DAY 5:

DAY 36 | EXODUS 19–20

MEMORY VERSES: EXODUS 20:1-3; GALATIANS 5:14

Following God's miraculous work to get His people out of Egypt, the Israelites journeyed through the desert, eventually setting up camp at Mount Sinai. On that mountain, God spoke to Moses, telling him that if the Israelites would remember what He had done and obey Him, they would demonstrate that they were His special and holy possession. God made good on His promise to Abraham to make a great nation out of Abraham's descendants, then He gave them a set of rules—the Ten Commandments—to help them know how to live as His chosen people. The first four focused on the people's relationship with God, while the next six focused on the people's relationships with one another. The ultimate goal of the Ten Commandments was to highlight humanity's need for God and point them toward holiness.

H

E

WEEK AT A GLANCE
Three months removed from Egypt, Israel found themselves in the wilderness of Sinai. During this time, God gave Moses the Ten Commandments and additional laws, as well as instructions for the building of the Tabernacle and its elements. I can't wait for you to dig in.

A

R

T

DAY 37 | EXODUS 24-25

MEMORY VERSES: EXODUS 20:1-3; GALATIANS 5:14

In Exodus 21–23 God gave the Israelites further instructions for worship and living. Then the Israelites made a covenant with God in which they promised to obey Him. The ritual sacrifice Moses performed to seal the covenant foreshadowed the death of Jesus on the cross—the animal's blood was shed as a sacrifice for the sins of the people, which made a way for them to unite with God in this covenant. Following the dictation of the law, God next laid out very specific instructions for the building of a tabernacle, a place set aside for His presence to dwell, in which they could regularly worship Him. Chapter 25 gives details for the ark, the table, and the lampstand. Each item was intentionally designed to point the worshipers to God, and they were made of a wide range of natural materials, meaning everyone was able to give an offering to help build the sanctuary (25:1-9). Giving is built into our relationship with God as an act of worship.

H

E

A

R

T

DID YOU KNOW?

All the elements of the original tabernacle point forward to Jesus:

• *The ark of the covenant and the mercy seat*—God's presence now dwells in believers through the Holy Spirit.

• *The table of showbread*—Jesus said He is the Bread of Life. The priests consumed this bread in the tabernacle. Today we consume the Word of God.

• *The lampstand*— Jesus said He is the Light of the world. The Holy Spirit enlightens us today.[4]

MEMORY VERSE

Pick one of the memory verse options for this week—Exodus 20:1-3; Galatians 5:14—and write the verse.

MEMORY VERSES: EXODUS 20:1-3; GALATIANS 5:14

DID YOU KNOW?

These elements of the tabernacle point forward to Jesus too:

• *Tabernacle structure*—God's presence dwells inside of us through the Holy Spirit.

• *The bronze altar*—Jesus is our ultimate and final sacrifice.

• *Courtyard*—We all have access to God through Jesus Christ and His righteousness.

• *Lampstand oil*—Jesus is the Light of the world, and as Christians we are to shine our light always.[5]

The tabernacle was a large tent used for gathering to worship. Because of the way God designed it, the tabernacle could be taken apart and carried as the people continued on their journey for the promised land. The tent served as a reminder of God's constant presence and their need to center life on Him, no matter where they went. The veil of the tabernacle, described in Exodus 26:31-35, separated the ark of the covenant and the mercy seat of God from the rest of the tabernacle and all the people. In other words, it separated the people from the presence of God. This is why it's so significant that when Jesus died on the cross, the veil was ripped in two (Luke 23:45). Jesus's sacrifice made access to God possible for all people, as it still does today.

H

E

A

R

T

DAY 39 | EXODUS 28-29

MEMORY VERSES: EXODUS 20:1-3; GALATIANS 5:14

Along with the instructions God gave Moses related to building the tabernacle and its components, He also provided instructions for the creation of the priestly garments—particularly the robes, ephod, and breastpiece worn by the high priest. Once the tabernacle had been constructed and furnished and the priestly garments had been created, everything needed to be dedicated and consecrated for worship. As part of that, God asked the people to give Him their best as an offering, and doing so became a regular part of their faith in and obedience to Him. As it did for the Israelites, giving God our best, not what's left, honors Him and shows our gratitude to Him for giving us His best through Christ.

DAILY CHALLENGE

What does giving God your best look like? What holds you back from offering your best to Him in worship? Prayerfully consider what God is calling you to sacrifice today.

MEMORY VERSE

Continue practicing the memory verse you chose. Write out as much of it as you can from memory, and then check to see how you did.

H

E

A

R

T

DAY 40 | EXODUS 30–31

MEMORY VERSES: EXODUS 20:1-3; GALATIANS 5:14

WEEK IN REVIEW

Spend some time reflecting on what you have learned this week. Record a truth from each day that you want to remember, or go back and highlight portions of your journal.

DAY 1:

DAY 2:

DAY 3:

DAY 4:

DAY 5:

As God wrapped up His instructions for the tabernacle, He described the Day of Atonement—one day a year in which the high priest made a sacrifice on behalf of the sins of all the Israelites. The writer of Hebrews tells us that the Day of Atonement pointed forward to the sacrifice of Jesus, whose death on the cross cleanses us from our sins once and for all (Heb. 9:24-28). Before appointing men to head up the building projects, God told the people to contribute money to the building project. God's final instruction to the people was a reminder not to work on the Sabbath. Building a place for worship was going to take a lot of work, but it did not exclude the people from worship itself.

H

E

A

R

T

DAY 41 | EXODUS 32-33

MEMORY VERSES: EXODUS 33:16; MATTHEW 22:37-39

The Israelites were guided by God's presence through the desert and heard Him speak to Moses on Mount Sinai, but even those awe-inspiring encounters with God did not keep them from sinning. Moses's prolonged absence from the Israelites—while he was on the mountain receiving instructions from God—led them to demand Aaron make a representation of God. Taking gold earrings from the women and children, Aaron made a golden calf, and the people held a great feast sacrificing to this idol. Like the people the apostle Paul condemned in Romans 1, the Israelites preferred to worship created things rather than the Creator Himself. In response to this sin, God threatened to destroy the people, but Moses interceded on their behalf, leading God to spare them. Our sin, too, warrants death, but Jesus interceded on our behalf, and the wrath that we earned was poured out on Him as He hung on the cross.

H

E

A

R

T

WEEK AT A GLANCE

Moses came down from meeting with God on the mountain and encountered a people who had lost their faith in God and His promises. However, God reaffirmed His covenant with Moses, and the people proceeded with the building of the tabernacle. Thank God He remains faithful even when we are faithless. Let's dive in!

DAY 42 | EXODUS 34–36:1

MEMORY VERSES: EXODUS 33:16; MATTHEW 22:37-39

THINK ABOUT IT

Make a list of your talents, gifts, skills, and abilities. All of these are gifts from God. Thank Him for giving you these.

Out of anger for the people's idolatry, Moses broke the first pair of stone tablets on which God had inscribed His Commandments. But as has been proved throughout Genesis and Exodus, God's faithfulness to His people is not based on their actions; it is rooted solely in His character. God renewed His covenant with Moses and inscribed a new set of tablets. When Moses ascended Mount Sinai again, God declared His name and nature, causing Moses to worship Him. In chapter 33 Moses asked to see God's glory, and on the mountain God granted him that request. When Moses came down from the mountain, his face shone with the light of God's glory. He then gathered the Israelites together, reminded them of God's laws, and put them to work building God's tabernacle. With this God's plans were in motion following the golden-calf diversion.

H

MEMORY VERSE

Pick one of the memory verse options for this week—Exodus 33:16; Matthew 22:37-39— and write the verse.

E

A

R

T

DAY 43 | EXODUS 40

MEMORY VERSES: EXODUS 33:16; MATTHEW 22:37-39

The Israelites assembled the tabernacle and all its components just as God instructed. It was a concerted effort on the part of Moses's leadership, the skill of numerous craftsmen, and the gifts of many people. After the tabernacle was constructed, Moses consecrated it and appointed Aaron and his sons as priests. Then God's glory filled the tabernacle, an act showing His approval of their obedience and His presence among them. Additionally, the cloud of God's glory in the temple became the guide for the Israelites' journey. The people had come a long way from their time as slaves in Egypt, despite their repeated sin and disobedience along the way.

DAILY CHALLENGE

Read Exodus 40:34-38 again. Spend some time with the Lord in quiet reflection. Then draw a picture, write a poem, or record a journal entry reflecting on the glory of the Lord.

H

E

A

R

T

DAY 44 | LEVITICUS 8-9

MEMORY VERSES: EXODUS 33:16; MATTHEW 22:37-39

THINK ABOUT IT

Our God is a God of second chances, as we see in Aaron's story and throughout the story of Israel. Write a prayer to God thanking Him for second, third, and fourth chances as you learn to live for Him.

MEMORY VERSE

Continue practicing the memory verse you chose. Write out as much of it as you can from memory, and then check to see how you did.

The tabernacle was a place where God's presence could dwell among His people. For this reason, the people needed to know how to live properly in His presence, which is the purpose of the book of Leviticus and the priesthood it describes. The role of a priest was one of a mediator between God and the people. God would speak to the people through the priests, and the priests would speak to God on behalf of the people. The priests also offered sacrifices to God on behalf of the people's sins. While the Levitical priests served God's purpose well during their time, they are a reminder for us that Jesus is the better priest, as Hebrews 7 describes. The Levitical priests were human. Therefore, each of them eventually died because of their sin. Their ability to atone for the people's sins was limited at best. As our great High Priest, however, Jesus is sinless and eternal, meaning His sacrifice is perfect and everlasting.

H

E

A

R

T

DAY 45 | LEVITICUS 16–17

MEMORY VERSES: EXODUS 33:16; MATTHEW 22:37-39

One of the most important parts of the priest's job was overseeing the Day of Atonement. This day was set aside as the only day of the year when the high priest could enter the holy of holies and appear before the ark of the covenant. On the Day of Atonement, the high priest offered sacrifices to seek God's forgiveness for the sins of the people. From the beginning, God has made a way for His sinful people to remain in fellowship with Him, even though they can do nothing to deserve it. The Day of Atonement served this purpose until the crucifixion of Jesus, at which time animal sacrifices for sins were no longer required thanks to the bodily sacrifice of Jesus Himself. Today God continues to draw His people back to Him when they sin through the conviction of the Holy Spirit. The Holy Spirit is the very presence of God living in every follower of Christ, and He guides us toward holiness and Christlikeness.

H

E

A

R

T

WEEK IN REVIEW

Spend some time reflecting on what you have learned this week. Record a truth from each day that you want to remember, or go back and highlight portions of your journal.

DAY 1:

DAY 2:

DAY 3:

DAY 4:

DAY 5:

DAY 46 | LEVITICUS 23

MEMORY VERSES: LEVITICUS 26:13; DEUTERONOMY 31:7-8

Part of God's plans for His covenant people included several festivals and holidays that served as a time for the people to gather together and worship God. All of the instructions God laid out for His people in Leviticus were intentional, and each of these festivals had important significance for their relationship with God. The Sabbath, which occurred weekly, was a day of rest and reflection meant to refocus the people's attention on God. The festivals celebrated God's redemption of His people from Egypt and His provisions for their physical and spiritual needs. The Day of Atonement constituted a day of self-denial in which the Israelites confessed their sins and the high priest made an atonement sacrifice. These special periods would also help the people remember God's acts of creation, deliverance, protection, and provision.

H

E

A

R

T

WEEK AT A GLANCE
This week we'll be reading about the Jewish festivals and holidays set up by God. As you read, take note of how each festival and holiday points to Jesus. We'll also read more about the Israelites' journey on the way to the promised land, Moses's leadership of God's people, and God's gracious kindness. God has much to show us this week!

DAY 47 | LEVITICUS 26

MEMORY VERSES: LEVITICUS 26:13; DEUTERONOMY 31:7-8

God reminded His people not to worship idols and to honor the Sabbath. He declared that obedience to His commands would bring blessing and life, while disobedience would bring curses and difficulties. If after disobeying His people repented and sought His forgiveness, they could again experience blessing and life. This cyclical pattern of obedience, blessing, disobedience, cursing, and redemption is the running theme throughout all of the Old Testament, and it's not until Jesus comes that the pattern is finally broken. God's favor is not dependent on our obedience. Because of Jesus's obedience, faith in Him is all that is necessary to have a relationship with God.

H

E

A

R

T

DAILY CHALLENGE
One of my favorite verses is Leviticus 26:13. Read it again. I remember what it is like to be in bondage. God broke those bars around my neck and enabled me to walk in freedom. Hallelujah! When did God break "the bars of your yoke," and how did that change you? Spend time praising God for His redemption and grace.

MEMORY VERSE
Pick one of the memory verse options for this week—Leviticus 26:13; Deuteronomy 31:7-8— and write the verse.

DAY 48 | NUMBERS 11-12

MEMORY VERSES: LEVITICUS 26:13; DEUTERONOMY 31:7-8

Numbers 12:3 says, "Moses was a very humble man, more so than anyone on the face of the earth." I have to think that Moses's humility was one of the keys to his leadership and sets an important example for us to follow, no matter where God has us leading.

The book of Numbers picks up with the story of the Israelites' journey from Egypt to the promised land where it left off in the book of Exodus. After the people built the tabernacle, they resumed their journey to the promised land, but their lack of faith in God again became evident when they complained about their condition. The complaints stirred up God's anger, but Moses interceded on behalf of the people, and God held back His anger. This unique relationship Moses had with God stirred up jealousy in his brother, Aaron, and his sister, Miriam. When Miriam criticized Moses's marriage and questioned his leadership, God struck her with leprosy, banishing her from the camp. However, Moses again interceded to God for her healing. Both of these accounts remind us of the human bent toward sinfulness and our need for an intercessor, whom we have in Jesus.

H

E

A

R

T

DAY 49 | NUMBERS 13–14

MEMORY VERSES: LEVITICUS 26:13; DEUTERONOMY 31:7-8

This passage describes the sending of twelve scouts into Canaan, the promised land, in preparation for invasion. Although God commanded the people to enter the land, ten of the spies returned with a negative report and warned the people not to enter because of the size and strength of the inhabitants. Only Joshua and Caleb urged the people to overcome their fears and to obey God's command to enter. As a result of the report, God punished the nation by declaring they would not be allowed to enter Canaan. One of the character traits of God made evident throughout the Old Testament is His justice, which is on display in this tragic scene. Because God is just, He could not allow a rebellious people to claim His blessing. Thankfully, faith in Jesus alone is enough to satisfy God's just wrath against our sin, but God still expects obedience from His people. We are able to obey Him through the empowerment of His Holy Spirit. Growing in obedience and trust is the focus of the Christian life and a pursuit that will take up the rest of our days.

THINK ABOUT IT

The Israelites complained and conspired against the Lord, and the text says their corpses would fall and their children would suffer the penalty and bear the consequences (Num. 14:26-35). That is a scary thought; it challenges us to consider what and who we may complain against. If this is a thought that feels convicting to you today, take some time to confess and ask the Lord for forgiveness.

MEMORY VERSE

Continue practicing the memory verse you chose. Write out as much of it as you can from memory, and then check to see how you did.

H

E

A

R

T

MEMORY VERSES: LEVITICUS 26:13; DEUTERONOMY 31:7-8

WEEK IN REVIEW

Spend some time reflecting on what you have learned this week. Record a truth from each day that you want to remember, or go back and highlight portions of your journal.

DAY 1:

DAY 2:

DAY 3:

DAY 4:

DAY 5:

As punishment for their disobedience, the Israelites would wander in the desert for forty years, and most would die there, never seeing the promised land. During their wandering years, their rebellion against God grew. Numbers 16–17 describes a rebellion that stirred up against Moses and Aaron's leadership, led by a Levite named Korah. The rebellion was stopped when God supernaturally destroyed the opponents and sent a plague among the Israelites as divine punishment. God then demonstrated His choice of Aaron and his descendants as priests. One of the most dangerous threats to a person's relationship with God is control or self-sufficiency. This dangerous thought causes us to think we know what is better for our lives and how to achieve it. Until we surrender complete control to God, we are unable to walk in the freedom and peace He offers.

H

E

A

R

T

DAY 51 | NUMBERS 20; 27:12-23

MEMORY VERSES: DEUTERONOMY 4:7; DEUTERONOMY 6:4-9

This point in Israel's story marks forty years since they escaped from slavery in Egypt. Just as God stated, most of the people died in the desert and never stepped foot in the promised land because of their disobedience. Unfortunately, the new generation of Israelites continued with their parents' pattern of rebellion against God for the lack of water at Kadesh. God gave Moses instructions to speak to the rock to bring water from it, but the people's grumbling drove him to strike the rock in impatience. Moses and Aaron failed to obey the Lord's instructions, thereby missing an opportunity to demonstrate their faith in God before the people. This failure to follow God's command, coupled with a rebellious and invective attitude against God's people, was a violation of the holiness of God, resulting in Moses being disqualified from entering the promised land. This account is a tragic realization that all of us are susceptible to sin. Numbers 27 reveals that Joshua was commissioned to succeed Moses and lead Israel into Canaan.

H

E

A

R

T

WEEK AT A GLANCE
We are now nearing the end of the Israelites' forty years of wilderness wandering and the promised land is on the horizon. During this time, Moses continued to teach the nation how to obey God and follow Him all the days of their lives.

DAY 52 | NUMBERS 34–35

MEMORY VERSES: DEUTERONOMY 4:7; DEUTERONOMY 6:4-9

DAILY CHALLENGE

After you finish today's reading and journaling, consider the following questions:

How would you benefit from the refuge God is offering you today in Christ?

What steps can you take to find refuge in Him?

.

MEMORY VERSE

Pick one of the memory verse options for this week—Deuteronomy 4:7; Deuteronomy 6:4-9—and write the verse.

The time for God's people to enter the promised land had come, just as God promised to Abraham, Isaac, and Jacob. God outlined in great detail how the land would be divided among the twelve tribes of Israel. God intentionally split up the Levites among all of the territories to serve as a reminder of their need for holiness, righteousness, and obedience. God also designated cities of refuge across the land as a place of escape and protection for a person who unintentionally murdered another person. The cities of refuge were more than just a place of retreat: they were a reminder of God's faithfulness to His people. Even today God invites all of us, no matter what we have done, to take refuge in Him. This was made possible by Jesus's life, death, and resurrection.

H

E

A

R

T

DAY 53 | DEUTERONOMY 1–2

MEMORY VERSES: DEUTERONOMY 4:7; DEUTERONOMY 6:4-9

At the beginning of the Israelites' journey to the promised land, God made a covenant with Moses that included the giving of the law. By the time the people reached the promised land, almost forty years had passed. Most of the original generation that left Egypt had died. Before the people inhabited the land, God reminded them of His expectations. In summary, this is the purpose of the book of Deuteronomy, which in large part is the record of Moses's speech to the people. Moses began his speech with a reminder to the people of what had taken place since leaving Egypt. Moses reiterated God's faithfulness. He desired for them to learn from the mistakes of their ancestors. Both Scripture and our relationships with other believers serve a similar purpose in our lives today. As we look back on how God has been faithful to His people throughout history, our own faith and trust in Him is strengthened.

DAILY CHALLENGE

Set aside some time today to write your own story of God's faithfulness, like Moses did for the people of Israel. As you reflect on your relationship with God, think of one person you can share your story with and then reach out to that person this week.

H

E

A

R

T

DAY 54 | DEUTERONOMY 3-4

MEMORY VERSES: DEUTERONOMY 4:7; DEUTERONOMY 6:4-9

In addition to reminding the Israelites of God's providence over their lives, Moses offered detailed instructions on how they were to live moving forward. What mattered most was that they remain faithful to God through obedience to His commands. Moses warned the people of the temptations idolatry presented. He encouraged them to teach each generation to obey the Lord. Keeping God's laws was essential to the people's prosperity and security. God promised that their wholehearted, consistent obedience would result in long lives in the land. Alternatively, if they disobeyed, they would experience the curses of divine discipline. Even today we demonstrate our love for God by obeying His ways, teaching younger generations about Him, and declaring the truths of His Word to the world.

DAILY CHALLENGE

God wanted the people to remember that He alone deserves first place in their lives. Make a list of the things that compete with the Lord for your time, attention, or loyalty, and ask Him to help you loosen your grip on each of these idols. Write down one action step you will take today to ensure God has first place in your life.

MEMORY VERSE

Continue practicing the memory verse you chose. Write out as much of it as you can from memory, and then check to see how you did.

H

E

A

R

T

DAY 55 | DEUTERONOMY 6–7

MEMORY VERSES: DEUTERONOMY 4:7; DEUTERONOMY 6:4-9

Deuteronomy 6 contains one of the most important passages in the Old Testament, the *Shema* (Deut. 6:4-9). These verses sum up what obedience to God looks like. Jesus referenced this text when He was asked what the greatest commandment was (Matt. 22:37-39). Moses instructed the people to love God with all their heart, soul, and strength. That single command encompassed all of the instructions of God. The idea was so important that they were told to teach their children this command, write it on doorposts, and make signs. By God's grace He had chosen the Israelites to be His people, and loving obedience was the only appropriate response to His grace. In chapter 7 God points out that He blessed the Israelites to be a blessing to those around them. Today God's chosen people are those who believe in His Son. Like the ancient Israelites, we are simply recipients of His grace, and He expects the same wholehearted love and obedience from us.

H

E

A

R

T

DAY 56 | DEUTERONOMY 8-9

MEMORY VERSES: JOSHUA 1:8-9; PSALM 1:1-2

As Moses continued in his speech to the Israelites, he warned them of the temptation to forget about God and their need for Him while prospering in their newfound land. Moses knew, as is true for us also, that when things are going well in life, it is easy to forget about our total dependency on God. Remembering God's great acts of deliverance from the past would be a way to keep their need for Him at the forefront of their minds. Moses also reminded the Israelites that they were undeserving recipients of God's grace, and the golden-calf episode was a glaring reminder of that truth. God's grace in their lives was based on His righteousness alone, as it is for God's children today. As the apostle Paul points out, "He made the one who did not know sin to be sin for us, so that in him we might become the righteousness of God" (2 Cor. 5:21).

H

WEEK AT A GLANCE

We'll read the final chapters of Deuteronomy and the beginning of the book of Joshua this week. Israel's journey of wandering drew to a close, and the conquest of the promised land was close. This week also highlights the transfer of leadership from Moses to Joshua, which marks the beginning of a new era for God's people. My heart is already racing in anticipation of these next few weeks! Let's get started.

E

A

R

T

DAY 57 | DEUTERONOMY 30–31

MEMORY VERSES: JOSHUA 1:8-9; PSALM 1:1-2

Deuteronomy 30 paints a vivid picture of God's mercy and grace against the rebellious heart of humanity—despite their patterns of rebellion. God promised to remain faithful to His covenant people. In Deuteronomy 30:11-20 Moses summarized the choice every person faces: the choice of life or death. Moses challenged the people to choose life, that is, to choose for themselves the path of life and blessing instead of the path of selfishness that leads to death. With that reminder, Moses handed the torch of leadership over to Joshua. Even for believers who have God's promise of forgiveness and eternal life, walking with Christ involves a continual, conscious choice of right over wrong, faithful obedience over selfish disobedience. Like the Israelites, we are called to choose the path of life.

DAILY CHALLENGE

Following God means a life of striving to live in obedience to His will and His commands. Read Deuteronomy 27–28 and make a list of blessings for obedience versus curses for disobedience.

H

E

MEMORY VERSE

Pick one of the memory verse options for this week—Joshua 1:8-9; Psalm 1:1-2—and write the verse.

A

R

T

THINK ABOUT IT

Think back over the life and ministry of Moses from your recent readings. What are your biggest takeaways that can be applied to your own relationship with God and the plans He has for you?

DAY 58 | DEUTERONOMY 32:48-52;34

MEMORY VERSES: JOSHUA 1:8-9; PSALM 1:1-2

The final chapters of Deuteronomy report Moses's final actions before passing the leadership baton to Joshua. Up to the very end of his life, Moses sought to live out the calling the Lord had given him at the burning bush. The book of Deuteronomy ends with a description of Moses as an unparalleled leader and prophet who had a relationship with God unlike any other. From the time of Moses, God's people looked forward to another Prophet who would come after Moses. Jesus Christ ultimately fulfilled that expectation. As Hebrews 3 tells us, Jesus is the true Savior who provided a way of redemption from sin, established the new covenant through His death on the cross for our sins, and thus had a greater glory than Moses.

H

E

A

R

T

DAY 59 | JOSHUA 1-2

MEMORY VERSES: JOSHUA 1:8-9; PSALM 1:1-2

After Moses's death God instructed Joshua to prepare the Israelites for entering the promised land. As Joshua faced the greatest challenge of his life, God reassured him about His continuing presence and challenged the new leader to show courage and to carefully follow God's instructions. In preparation for entering Canaan, Joshua sent two men to scout the city of Jericho. The men found refuge from Rahab, a prostitute whose house was located on the city wall. Rahab heard about the God of the Israelites and understood He was unique, and that motivated her to action. Before the Israelites even entered Canaan, God was making His glory known among the people there. Rahab not only expressed her faith in God verbally, she also acted in ways that demonstrated her faith in God was genuine. Hebrews 11:31 points to Rahab as an example of heroic faith.

H

E

A

R

T

DID YOU KNOW?

Three times God told Joshua to be strong and courageous:

- Because God had promised to give the land (1:6)
- Because of God's word (1:7)
- Because of God's presence going with them (1:9)

Be praying for the courage and strength to put feet to your faith today. Pray that like Joshua and Rahab, your faith will be an example for many.

MEMORY VERSE

Continue practicing the memory verse you chose. Write out as much of it as you can from memory, and then check to see how you did.

DAY 60 | JOSHUA 3-4

MEMORY VERSES: JOSHUA 1:8-9; PSALM 1:1-2

WEEK IN REVIEW

Spend some time reflecting on what you have learned this week. Record a truth from each day that you want to remember, or go back and highlight portions of your journal.

DAY 1:

DAY 2:

DAY 3:

DAY 4:

DAY 5:

Joshua 3–4 describes the moment the Israelites had been waiting for since they crossed the Red Sea and escaped the Egyptians—the crossing into the promised land. After a forty-year diversion because of their unfaithfulness, the moment finally came. Just as God miraculously enabled them to cross the Red Sea, He again enabled them to cross the Jordan River on dry land. The two river crossings show God's consistent presence with and protection of His people. After the crossing, Joshua instructed one man from each tribe to gather a stone for erecting a memorial. That memorial served as a reminder of God's faithfulness and power for the Israelites and future generations. God continues to work miracles in the lives of His children today, not the least of which is the gift of salvation that none of us deserve. Taking the time to reflect on God's gifts and miraculous works is a vital part of a relationship with Him.

H

E

A

R

T

DAY 61 | JOSHUA 5:10-15; 6

MEMORY VERSES: JOSHUA 24:14-15; JUDGES 2:12

After God led the Israelites across the Jordan safely, they found themselves in a position to claim the promised land, which would happen through a series of military conquests as they conquered Canaan's major cities. The first city to be attacked was Jericho, but before Joshua could formulate a plan, he received a visit from a heavenly messenger who gave him instructions on how to overtake it. Noticeably absent from the plan was any military strategy; Jericho would be overtaken by trust and obedience alone. God was clearly in control of this situation. Joshua needed to display trust in God's plan by following His instructions. On the seventh day, the people marched around the city seven times, blew trumpets, and shouted. Then God intervened miraculously. He delivered the city into the Israelites' hands, all except for Rahab and her family, whom He had promised to protect because she helped God's people. We must always remember that our God keeps His promises. He is who He says He is and does what He says He will do.

H

E

A

R

T

WEEK AT A GLANCE
Ladies, you've now been reading consistently in your Bible for three months! You're well on your way to creating a healthy spiritual discipline that could last for a lifetime. Keep it up! As we finish Joshua and begin Judges, we'll encounter the full conquest of the promised land and the devastating effect the passing of another amazing leader of God had on the nation of Israel.

DAY 62 | JOSHUA 7-8

THINK ABOUT IT

Achan coveted what didn't belong to him. He confiscated and concealed the devoted items. However, God revealed Achan's sin because no one can hide from Him. The allure of sin isn't worth what you have to endure after. Reflect on times when this has proven true in your life, then take some time to confess today's sins God.

One of the instructions God gave His people as they overtook Jericho was not to seize any wealth or treasures of the Canaanites. God orchestrated this conquest, and the goal was bringing glory to His name, but a focus on material gain would distract the people from this goal. One man, Achan, violated God's instruction, and his greed had a devastating impact on him, his family, and the community as a whole. After this sin was brought to light and dealt with, Joshua was able to lead the people in a successful conquest of their next city, Ai. Joshua knew this takeover, like Jericho, only happened because God allowed it to, so he responded in worship and a renewal of the covenant with God. The opportunity God gave the Israelites for a second chance to conquer Ai, despite Achan's disobedience, is a reminder for us of God's grace and willingness to restore those He loves. When we address our sins through confession and repentance, God is quick to forgive us and restore us to a right relationship with Him.

H

E

MEMORY VERSE

Pick one of the memory verse options for this week—Joshua 24:14-15; Judges 2:12—and write the verse.

A

R

T

DAY 63 | JOSHUA 23-24

MEMORY VERSES: JOSHUA 24:14-15; JUDGES 2:12

Chapters 9–22 of Joshua describe the conquering of the promised land and the Israelites' settling in that land. The book ends with Joshua's farewell address to the people, in which he reminded them of God's power and faithfulness to His promises and their need to be strong in faith, obedient to the covenant, and loyal to God. Joshua recapped how God had proved Himself faithful to them and His covenant from as far back as the time of Abraham. Joshua's address closed with a challenge to the people to renew their commitment to and worship of God alone, and the people accepted. Like the Israelites, we live in a world with many influences that might sway us from exclusive devotion to Christ. Joshua's challenge reminds us that if we hope to devote our lives exclusively to the Lord, we must hear and obey the Word of God and renew our commitment to Him every day.

DAILY CHALLENGE

Today's reading from Joshua emphasizes wholehearted devotion to God alone. Spend time in prayer, confessing all the various things in your life that steal your allegiance away from God. Ask for the Spirit's help in identifying those distractions, and renew your commitment to Him today.

H

E

A

R

T

MEMORY VERSES: JOSHUA 24:14-15; JUDGES 2:12

DID YOU KNOW?

The stories of the judges follow this cycle:

- Sin—They worshiped idols.
- Slavery—They were oppressed by their enemies.
- Supplication—They cried out to God to save them.
- Salvation—God raised up a judge to deliver them.
- Stillness—While the judge was alive, Israel would have peace and follow the Lord. When the judge died, the people would return to idol worship and the sin cycle started all over.

MEMORY VERSE

Continue practicing the memory verse you chose. Write out as much of it as you can from memory, and then check to see how you did.

The book of Judges continues the story of Israel's efforts to take control of the promised land following the death of their leader, Joshua. From the start, it becomes evident that with Joshua's death the nation started to drift astray, despite the commitment to God they had made before Joshua's death. Judges 2:10 reveals the shocking truth that a new generation of Israelites arose who did not know God and did not remember His works among their people. This new generation disobeyed God and abandoned the covenant of their fathers. In turn, God's judgment came down on them through military defeats and oppression by other people groups. After this oppression had gone on for several years, the people finally called out to God for mercy, and as He had done countless times before, God delivered them, this time through Othniel, the first of His appointed judges—the new form of leadership God put in place. This pattern of sin, oppression, repentance, and deliverance through a new judge continues throughout the book, and it paints a clear picture of humanity's bent toward sin and God's inexhaustible love.

H

E

A

R

T

DAY 65 | JUDGES 4

MEMORY VERSES: JOSHUA 24:14-15; JUDGES 2:12

When the Israelites again turned to evil, God allowed them to be oppressed by a Canaanite king for twenty years, at which point they finally cried out for deliverance again. God heard their cries, and He responded by appointing Deborah as their new judge. In addition to being a judge, Deborah was also a prophet who delivered God's messages to the Israelites. She served as God's spiritual spokesperson to Barak, who was Israel's military leader. God used the joint efforts of Deborah and Barak to defeat the Canaanite forces that oppressed His people. Deborah stands out as one of the godly leaders in Israel's history. She listened and obeyed the words of God, had faith in His ability to work through her, and encouraged the ways God was working in other people. Deborah also modeled what Jesus would later confirm: we demonstrate our love for God and obedience to Him through a life of service to others.

H

E

A

R

T

WEEK IN REVIEW
Spend some time reflecting on what you have learned this week. Record a truth from each day that you want to remember, or go back and highlight portions of your journal.

DAY 1:

DAY 2:

DAY 3:

DAY 4:

DAY 5:

DAY 66 | JUDGES 6-7

MEMORY VERSES: PSALM 19:14; GALATIANS 4:4-5

After the spiritual high and forty years of peace that came with Deborah's leadership, the Israelites again relapsed into idol worship, and God allowed them to suffer oppression for seven years. When the Israelites cried out for help, God called a young farmer named Gideon to deliver them. The first thing revealed about Gideon was his fear, something that would plague him throughout his leadership. In fear Gideon requested two signs of assurance that he truly was speaking with God, which God supplied. The great test of Gideon's leadership came when God called him into battle against the Midianites, but then reduced the army to just a few hundred men. As God had done in the battle of Jericho, He again reminded the people that His presence was all they needed, and they could trust Him to be their Deliverer. We do not need signs from God today to know that He continues to faithfully deliver His people from the oppression of sin. God made His role as Deliverer glaringly clear when He sent His own Son to the cross to deliver His people from sin and death once and for all.

H

E

A

R

T

WEEK AT A GLANCE

This week we'll continue in the book of Judges with the stories of Gideon and Samson, and we'll finish the week with a favorite of mine, Ruth! Believe it or not, you're almost at the halfway point of the Old Testament reading portion of our reading plan. I hope the puzzle pieces of God's big story are coming together for you. Understanding the Old Testament gives us a better appreciation of the New Testament and the hope of the gospel found in Jesus.

DAY 67 | JUDGES 13–14

MEMORY VERSES: PSALM 19:14; GALATIANS 4:4-5

Another spiritual regression by the Israelites brought yet another judge onto the scene—Samson. To set Samson apart for God's work, he was bound by the Nazirite vow even before his birth, which meant he couldn't cut his hair, touch a corpse or carcass of a dead animal, or consume alcohol. Furthermore, the Spirit of God gave Samson extraordinary strength. Unfortunately, as chapter 14 reveals, Samson failed to remember and keep God's commands; instead, he gave in to the passions and lusts of the world and married a Philistine woman, something specifically outlawed by God. Early on, we see hints that pride and self-indulgence would be Samson's downfalls. Samson's story reminds us that humility is one of the most important virtues in the kingdom of God. With a healthy, balanced view of ourselves in relation to God, we put ourselves in a position to be used by God and to reflect His humility and love to the world.

DAILY CHALLENGE

Control is a struggle for most women. In our careers, parenting, marriages, friendships, social media images, and on and on, we constantly fight against a need to control as much as we can. Whether your drive for control is rooted in pride, anxiety, or a mix of both, it's not God's best for you. He is the only one with the wisdom and power to control your life, so let Him! Identify an area where you have a false sense of control and one thing you can do today to hand that over to God.

MEMORY VERSE

Pick one of the memory verse options for this week—Psalm 19:14; Galatians 4:4-5—and write the verse.

H

E

A

R

T

DAY 68 | JUDGES 15–16

MEMORY VERSES: PSALM 19:14; GALATIANS 4:4-5

THINK ABOUT IT

What fear, struggle, or sin do you need to take to God in prayer? What is weighing on your heart today? Write a prayer to God, and be open and honest in your communication with Him.

During a time of separation from his wife, Samson discovered that her father had given her in marriage to another man. Exacting revenge, Samson killed one thousand Philistine men with the jawbone of a donkey. Later, Samson fell in love with a woman named Delilah, whom Philistine leaders bribed to uncover the secret of Samson's strength so they could capture, humiliate, and kill him, which she did. When Delilah shaved off Samson's braids, the Spirit left him, and he lost the true source of his strength—God Himself. Samson was then captured and blinded by the Philistines. Still hoping to conquer the Philistines, Samson prayed to the Lord for strength, and his prayer was answered. While God was dishonored by Samson's sinful behavior, God nevertheless honored the calling He had given Samson. God is always faithful to the calling and gifts with which He equips us to serve Him. He faithfully responds to our faith, however weak and confused we may be: "If we are faithless, he remains faithful, for he cannot deny himself" (2 Tim. 2:13).

H

E

A

R

T

DAY 69 | RUTH 1-2

MEMORY VERSES: PSALM 19:14; GALATIANS 4:4-5

During the time of the judges, a severe famine broke out in Israel, so an Israelite man named Elimelech moved with his wife, Naomi, and two sons from Bethlehem in Judah to the land of Moab. While there, Elimelech died, both sons married Moabite women, and then both sons also died. Naomi decided to return to her home in Judah, and Ruth chose to go with her, a choice that revealed her love, her loyalty, and her undying commitment to Naomi. Ruth even went so far as to pledge allegiance to Naomi's God. Once in Bethlehem, Ruth took the initiative to help provide for Naomi by gleaning in the nearby grain fields. In the process, Ruth was noticed and befriended by a man named Boaz, one of Naomi's relatives who provided the two widows with grain and protection in a generous display of kindness. The story of Ruth is the story of God's providential love on display— a love that extends to all people who have faith in Him.

MEMORY VERSE

Continue practicing the memory verse you chose. Write out as much of it as you can from memory, and then check to see how you did.

H

E

A

R

T

DAY 70 | RUTH 3-4

MEMORY VERSES: PSALM 19:14; GALATIANS 4:4-5

WEEK IN REVIEW

Spend some time reflecting on what you have learned this week. Record a truth from each day that you want to remember, or go back and highlight portions of your journal.

DAY 1:

DAY 2:

DAY 3:

DAY 4:

DAY 5:

Boaz's commitment to Ruth and Naomi unfolds in Ruth 3–4. With Naomi's guidance, Ruth approached Boaz and asked him to be her family redeemer—a relative who took on the responsibility of caring for a woman after her husband died. Without a redeemer, the widow would be left destitute in a society that did not make it easy on widows to prosper. In response to Ruth's request, Boaz followed the process for becoming her redeemer, and the two eventually married. By giving Ruth a husband and a son, the Lord graciously redeemed Ruth's seemingly hopeless situation. The story of Ruth and Boaz reminds us of the gospel, when Jesus Christ came to earth to be our Redeemer. We were born into the hopelessness of sin, but through the death and resurrection of Jesus, God redeems us, He buys us back into His family, and He secures our eternal future with Him.

H

E

A

R

T

DAY 71 | 1 SAMUEL 1-2

MEMORY VERSES: 1 SAMUEL 15:22; 1 SAMUEL 16:7

During the time of the judges, Israel reached a spiritual low point. The priesthood was corrupt, as the behavior of Eli's sons reveals, and many people turned away from the faith of their forefathers. However, from the beginning of 1 Samuel, it becomes evident that a remnant of faithful Israelites still remained. First Samuel 1–2 describes the fervent prayers of Hannah, a faithful woman who was desperate for a child. Hannah pled with God to give her a son who, in return, she would give back to Him in commitment to His service. God answered Hannah's prayer. She gave birth to Samuel, who was dedicated to God for a lifetime of service as she promised. Samuel was the last judge of Israel, and to this day his mother is an example of the self-sacrificial nature God expects from His children.

H

E

A

R

T

WEEK AT A GLANCE
This week begins our reading in 1 Samuel, where we'll camp out for this week and next. We'll read the prayer of a broken woman, the Israelites' demand for a king other than God, the choosing of that king, and a return to conflict for the nation of Israel. Let's see what happens.

DAY 72 | 1 SAMUEL 3; 8

MEMORY VERSES: 1 SAMUEL 15:22; 1 SAMUEL 16:7

DAILY CHALLENGE

God calls us all to something. What has He called you to during this season in your life? Illustrate a picture or write out a description of that calling. Put your drawing or description somewhere you will see it often, and use it as a reminder to commit yourself to the calling God has given you.

From the time he was a little boy, Samuel served as an apprentice to Eli, the priest. During this time, God called Samuel to a life of prophetic ministry. While resting near the ark, Samuel heard the Lord speak to him. God took the initiative, as He always does, and after some confusion about whose voice he heard, Samuel submitted to God. Without yet knowing what God was specifically asking, Samuel enlisted himself into service. Over the years Samuel continued to grow in his relationship with God and his responsibilities to the nation during a transitional and unstable time in their history. The people voiced their desire to be more like their neighboring nations, who were all ruled by kings, and they hoped that becoming a monarchy would give them strength against their enemies. So they asked Samuel to appoint a king to govern them—a request that flew in the face of their identity as God's chosen people, set apart from all other nations. God granted their request but considered it simply another of the many rebellious choices of Israel.

H

E

MEMORY VERSE

Pick one of the memory verse options for this week—1 Samuel 15:22; 1 Samuel 16:7—and write the verse.

A

R

T

MEMORY VERSES: 1 SAMUEL 15:22; 1 SAMUEL 16:7

The Israelites rebelled against God by demanding a king, and Samuel, with God's approval, granted their request. Even though a monarchy was not God's desire for the people, God still took it upon Himself to select who would be the nation's first king. God worked through a series of seemingly unrelated events to reveal who that king would be. Saul, in the process of searching for some lost donkeys, solicited the help of Samuel. All of this happened according to God's predicted plan, which revealed to Samuel that Saul was God's appointed leader. From the beginning of Saul's story, though, we see hints of the lifelong struggle that would plague his leadership—a lack of trust in God (9:21; 10:22). Saul's life is a sad story of unrealized potential, but it's an important reminder of God's desire that we trust Him and His plans for our lives, resulting in our unwavering devotion.

DID YOU KNOW?

God knew one day the Israelites would reject Him as king and ask for another. He gave instructions about the kingship back in Deuteronomy 17:14-20, approximately four hundred years before Saul was appointed. God knows our future better than we know our own past.[7]

H

E

A

R

T

DAY 74 | 1 SAMUEL 13–14

MEMORY VERSES: 1 SAMUEL 15:22; 1 SAMUEL 16:7

THINK ABOUT IT

Reflect on the attitudes and actions of Saul in these two chapters. What do you learn from him about how not to approach your relationship with God? Furthermore, what do you learn about God from this portion of Israel's history?

One of the consequences of Israel's new monarchy was a renewed conflict with the Philistines, Israel's enemy neighbor. Saul experienced military victory, which encouraged the people in their ability to fight back against the Philistines. First Samuel 13–14 draws a comparison between the leadership of Saul and Jonathan, Saul's son and commander of half of Israel's army. Saul was consumed by his own selfish goals, to the point that he ignored God's instruction and usurped the role of priest, offering a sacrifice that displeased God. This pattern of disobedience would lead to an abrupt end to Saul's reign, when he would be replaced by David, "a man after [God's] own heart" (1 Sam. 13:14). Jonathan, on the other hand, acknowledged trust in God's power and leadership, seeking confirmation from God before acting. The lives of these two men are a reminder that what you believe about God determines the actions you take in your relationship with Him.

MEMORY VERSE

Continue practicing the memory verse you chose. Write out as much of it as you can from memory, and then check to see how you did.

H

E

A

R

T

DAY 75 | 1 SAMUEL 15–16

MEMORY VERSES: 1 SAMUEL 15:22; 1 SAMUEL 16:7

Saul's repeated disobedience had disastrous consequences for him and his family. God equated Saul's failure to obey with idolatry, and for that, he would remove him as king. This set the stage for David, who would go down in history as Israel's greatest king. In 1 Samuel 13:14 Samuel described the next king as a man after God's own heart, but very little else is told about David other than his unassuming build and his work as a shepherd. That didn't matter, though, because God chose him to be king and anointed him with His Holy Spirit, and those were the only qualifications that mattered. The same is true of God's people today: God has chosen you to serve Him, and He has equipped you for that task by giving you the presence of His very Spirit. The Holy Spirit is committed to making you, like David, into a person after God's own heart, and all you have to do is surrender in order to allow Him to do so.

WEEK IN REVIEW

Spend some time reflecting on what you have learned this week. Record a truth from each day that you want to remember, or go back and highlight portions of your journal.

DAY 1:

DAY 2:

DAY 3:

DAY 4:

DAY 5:

H

E

A

R

T

DAY 76 | 1 SAMUEL 17-18

MEMORY VERSES: 1 SAMUEL 17:46-47; 2 TIMOTHY 4:17A

The story of David and Goliath is one of the most well-known encounters in Scripture. The Philistine army challenged the Israelite army to a battle between their greatest champions. The Philistine champion was the giant Goliath, whose presence was so foreboding, no Israelite wanted the seemingly impossible challenge of battling him. David (who was simply delivering lunch to his older brothers in the army) was offended by the mockery Goliath hurled against Israel's God, so he used his slingshot and the power of God Himself to defend God's honor and kill the giant. Chapter 18 goes on to tell how, in the aftermath of his victory over Goliath, David's life changed both for the better and for the worse—he discovered a lasting friend in Jonathan and a bitter rival in Saul. David's defeat of the giant Goliath is a great biblical account, but it's more than that—it's also a picture of the gospel. In Christ we have an even greater King than David—a King who defeated the giants of sin and death in order to set His people free.

H

E

A

R

T

WEEK AT A GLANCE

This week we'll be moving further into the kingdom period of Israel's history. King Saul was rejected because of his disobedience. David was the newly anointed king who waited for his chance to take the throne. Our first day's reading is the battle between David and Goliath, which may be familiar to you. If so, ask the Lord to give you fresh eyes as you read this familiar account.

MEMORY VERSES: 1 SAMUEL 17:46-47; 2 TIMOTHY 4:17A

Saul's jealousy of David's accomplishments drove him mad, so he ordered David's death. However, Jonathan warned David, and he escaped. Once again, Jonathan stands out as a model for believers today. Jonathan understood that God had appointed David to be the next king, and he knew his father's actions did not bring honor to God. Even though Saul was Jonathan's father, Jonathan was submissive first and foremost to the Lord. No one had a greater claim on Jonathan's life than God. David and Jonathan solidified their friendship with a covenant of loyalty to one another and to God. As Jesus teaches in the great commandment, loyalty and submission to God are to take first priority in the life of a Christian, but this also naturally encompasses loving others, as Jonathan modeled so well.

THINK ABOUT IT

Jonathan is best known for his friendship with David. First Samuel 18:1 declares that Jonathan's life "was bound to David in close friendship"—a phrase also used to describe the pledge Judah made to protect Benjamin (Gen. 44:30).[8] Who has the Lord tied together with you for the purpose of His mission?

MEMORY VERSE

Pick one of the memory verse options for this week—
1 Samuel 17:46-47;
2 Timothy 4:17a—and write the verse.

H

E

A

R

T

DAY 78 | 1 SAMUEL 21–22

MEMORY VERSES: 1 SAMUEL 17:46-47; 2 TIMOTHY 4:17A

READ ON

David was on the run for quite awhile because Saul was searching for him. For additional reading of what this time was like for David, read these psalms:

- Psalm 22 (in tomorrow's reading)
- Psalm 52
- Psalm 56
- Psalm 57
- Psalm 142

Although parts of David's life give a clear foreshadowing of Christ, it doesn't take long for us to be reminded that David was still a sinful human being whom God chose to use for His glory. David fled into exile because Saul wanted to kill him, and during that time, he made a series of selfish decisions that revealed his lack of faith that God would protect him and bring him into power as He had promised. David's actions had a devastating impact on Ahimelech and eighty-five other priests who were all murdered by Saul for the role Ahimelech played in assisting David. One of the things that makes David a hero of our faith is his example of repentance—when David learned of these deaths, he acknowledged his sin and attempted to make it right. Throughout his life, David would sin many times, sometimes with tragic consequences, but he always repented and returned to the Lord. Even more importantly, God always accepted him back and continued to use David to make His name known. Like David, we often sin, but God is quick to forgive us and shower us with His grace when we repent of our sins and return to Him.

H

E

A

R

T

DAY 79 | PSALM 22; 1 SAMUEL 24–25:1

MEMORY VERSES: 1 SAMUEL 17:46-47; 2 TIMOTHY 4:17A

During his life David penned many of the psalms that are now included in the book of Psalms. One of those, Psalm 22, came from a time in David's life when he found himself in great despair. David knew the plans God had for his life, but at that moment, they felt unattainable, and God felt absent. However, by the end of his prayer, David's pleas turned to praise, and he acknowledged that although God felt far away, David knew He was not. While we don't know from what specific circumstances this psalm stemmed, David's experience in 1 Samuel 24 parallels it well. Saul's pursuit of David forced him into hiding in a cave, an isolated place that undoubtedly felt helpless, but when presented with the opportunity to kill Saul, David did not. In that moment, David chose to claim God's promises for his life and his future, and to trust God to bring them to fruition. This is the same example Jesus gave us on the cross when He echoed David's cry—"My God, my God, why have you abandoned me?" (Ps. 22:1)—but even so, both Jesus and David surrendered their very lives to the plans of their Father.

H

E

A

R

T

DAILY CHALLENGE

Take some time to reread Psalm 22 slowly. Then read Matthew 27:11-54. Take note of all the parallels between David's words and Jesus's words on the cross.

MEMORY VERSE

Continue practicing the memory verse you chose. Write out as much of it as you can from memory, and then check to see how you did.

MEMORY VERSES: 1 SAMUEL 17:46-47; 2 TIMOTHY 4:17A

WEEK IN REVIEW

Spend some time reflecting on what you have learned this week. Record a truth from each day that you want to remember, or go back and highlight portions of your journal.

DAY 1:

DAY 2:

DAY 3:

DAY 4:

DAY 5:

These final chapters of Saul's story tell a tragic end to his life and reveal the consequences of his failure to trust God, just as his early years foreshadowed. After years of failing to listen to God, God finally quit speaking to Saul. When confronted with a new threat from the Philistines, Saul approached a medium—a witch—in hopes that she could speak with Samuel's spirit and get him the spiritual wisdom he needed for this battle. This act was done in direct disobedience to the laws of God—laws Saul had previously sought to uphold by banning the practice of mediums altogether. Through the power of God, Samuel did speak to Saul, and his words summarized Saul's great failure in life: "You did not obey the LORD" (1 Sam. 28:18). Samuel then predicted what chapter 31 proved to be true: the Philistines would defeat the Israelites, and Saul and his sons would die in the battle. What Samuel didn't reveal, though, is that Saul would take his own life. From beginning to end, Saul's life shows us the missed opportunities and spiritual unrest of a person who refuses to live in submission to God.

H

E

A

R

T

WEEK 17

DAY 81 | 2 SAMUEL 1; 2:1-7

MEMORY VERSES: PSALM 23:1-3; PSALM 51:10-13

In 1 Samuel 16 God chose David as the one who would replace Saul as king; and after many years of tension, wars, Saul's downfall, and David's patience, the time for David to take over the throne finally arrived. However, that time in David's life was not particularly joyful, for it was marked with grief over the deaths of Saul and Jonathan. David sang a lament to express his sadness, and that same lament became part of the nation's collective grieving for the loss of their king. David's lament marks a transition in the narrative from Saul's life to David's, which remains the focus for the rest of 2 Samuel. When the time of mourning for Saul and Jonathan was over, David asked the Lord to show him what to do next— a question that revealed his reliance upon God and his desire to live out his calling as God's anointed ruler. There was no question that David would be a much different king than Saul was and that David was the one whose obedience we should seek to emulate instead.

H

E

A

R

T

WEEK AT A GLANCE

Saul's term as king ended with his death and his sons' deaths. David's rise to the throne began, but it would not be easy. This week we'll read about his rise to power and about a personal downfall in David's life.

DAY 82 | 2 SAMUEL 3:1; 5; PSALM 23

DID YOU KNOW?

David was thirty years old when he was anointed king of Judah. He was anointed three times total in his life:

1 Samuel 16:13—The prophet Samuel anointed David as future king.

2 Samuel 2:4—The men of Judah anointed him king over the house of Judah. He reigned over Judah alone for seven years and six months.

2 Samuel 5—The remaining tribes of Israel came together and anointed him as their king at Jerusalem. He reigned over both Judah and all Israel for thirty-three years, which make a total of a forty-year reign.

MEMORY VERSE

Pick one of the memory verse options for this week—Psalm 23:1-3; Psalm 51:10-13—and write the verse.

David's rise to power was not without conflict and tension between those loyal to him and those who were still loyal to Saul, but David was God's chosen leader. Because of this, eventually he did become king. After several military victories and the establishment of his palace in Jerusalem, David realized that the source of his success was the Lord. God had been preparing David to be the king of Israel, and His providential concern for His people was evident through David's actions. Second Samuel 5:10 notes an important truth that weaved throughout David's life story: "David became more and more powerful, and the LORD God of Armies was with him." David recognized God's presence and power was at the root of his success, something he reflected on in Psalm 23. No matter what David went through, he acknowledged that God was his Shepherd who would always be by his side. As David reminds us, God has promised to do whatever it takes to lead, guide, and protect us, and the very cross of Christ assures us that He will do just that.

H

E

A

R

T

DAY 83 | 2 SAMUEL 6-7

MEMORY VERSES: PSALM 23:1-3; PSALM 51:10-13

As one of his first actions after acquiring Jerusalem and making it his capital, David moved the ark of the covenant to the city. God's laws contained specific instructions for carrying the ark, but the men moving it failed to follow that law, and one man died as a result. The setback caused David to reconsider his plans, and also opened his eyes to the holiness of God. After a three-month delay, he finally completed moving the ark to Jerusalem. Next David planned a temple to house the ark, but God stopped him in the process. Even though David's motive was good, his desire was not in line with God's purpose or timetable. Construction on the temple would have to wait another generation. God did, however, make an eternal covenant with David that promised his kingdom would endure forever. The New Testament writers help us understand that the promises of the covenant with David were ultimately fulfilled in Jesus Christ, our eternal King (Acts 2:22-36).

DID YOU KNOW?

David's reign was one of fighting. Solomon's reign was one of building. Through both of these men, God promised to establish their kingdom forever. Jesus Christ is the fulfillment of that promise.

PROMISE

- 2 Samuel 7:12-16
- Isaiah 11:1
- Jeremiah 23:5-6

FULFILLMENT

- Matthew 1:1
- Luke 1:32-33
- Acts 15:15-16
- Hebrews 1:5

H

E

A

R

T

DAY 84 | PSALM 18; 2 SAMUEL 9

MEMORY VERSES: PSALM 23:1-3; PSALM 51:10-13

DAILY CHALLENGE

Psalm 18 is flooded with truths about God. Make a list of various aspects of God's nature you find. I'll get you started:

- God's way is perfect (v. 30).

- God gives strength and security (vv. 32-33).

-

-

-

MEMORY VERSE

Continue practicing the memory verse you chose. Write out as much of it as you can from memory, and then check to see how you did.

One of the highlights of David's friendship with Jonathan was the time when Jonathan helped protect David from Saul's wrath. In response to that kindness, David made a promise with Jonathan to always show kindness to Jonathan's descendants. Now as king, David had the chance to make good on that promise by giving Mephibosheth—Jonathan's son—all of Saul's remaining property, inviting him to live under the protection of the palace. Jonathan had shown grace to David, so David extended that same grace to Mephibosheth. David's understanding of the character of God, which is elaborated on in Psalm 18, motivated the love and grace he showed Mephibosheth. This story from David's time as king gives us an incredible illustration of the gospel in action. God has extended His grace to us by inviting us into His family through the salvation available in Christ. Once we accept God's gift of grace and become His children, He expects us to reflect His love and grace to the world in return.

H

E

A

R

T

DAY 85 | 2 SAMUEL 11–12

MEMORY VERSES: PSALM 23:1-3; PSALM 51:10-13

Second Samuel 11–12 tells the infamous account of David's adultery with Bathsheba, as well as the sinful actions and devastating consequences that followed. While David was God's anointed king who God described as a man after His own heart, he was still very human with fully human temptations and desires. David had an affair with Bathsheba, a woman who was married to a man in David's army. The affair led to a pregnancy, which David attempted to cover up. When the cover-up didn't go as David planned, David had Bathsheba's husband murdered in battle, which highlights the destructive pattern of sin David was trapped in. David tried to keep his sin a secret, but God used the prophet Nathan to expose David's sin and move him toward confession and repentance. This story highlights the devastating consequences of sin in our lives and our relationships, but it also reveals the great lengths God goes to in order to bring us back to Him. Ultimately, this story is a reminder that while David was a great king, Jesus is the true and better King whose sinless, perfect life makes our own victory over sin possible.

H

E

A

R

T

WEEK IN REVIEW
Spend some time reflecting on what you have learned this week. Record a truth from each day that you want to remember, or go back and highlight portions of your journal.

DAY 1:

DAY 2:

DAY 3:

DAY 4:

DAY 5:

DAY 86 | PSALM 51

MEMORY VERSES: PSALM 1:1-6; PSALM 119:9-11

David wrote Psalm 51 after Nathan confronted him about his sins with Bathsheba and toward Uriah (2 Sam. 11–12). This psalm records David's cry to God for forgiveness, including his confession of sin, his plea for God's cleansing, his acknowledgment of God's holiness, and his request that God restore joy to David's life and blessing to Jerusalem. This psalm is an example for us of genuine sorrow over sin and the kind of repentant heart God desires. David's life reminds us that God is ready and willing to forgive repentant sinners completely and restore them to fellowship with Him. What matters to God is a truly "broken and humbled heart" (Ps. 51:17). This attitude toward sin ushers in God's grace and forgiveness.

H

E

A

R

T

WEEK AT A GLANCE

We start out this week with one of my favorite passages in all of Scripture. Psalm 51 was written in the aftermath of some of the most sinful times of David's life. We'll continue reading various psalms that David wrote as he reflected on key moments in his life.

DAY 87 | 2 SAMUEL 24; PSALM 24

MEMORY VERSES: PSALM 1:1-6; PSALM 119:9-11

The last chapter of 2 Samuel continues the theme of God's blessing on David's life and the nation of Israel because of His faithfulness to His covenant. However, the events in this chapter are another example of God temporarily removing His blessing because of sin. The military census David took angered God because it happened at a time when the nation of Israel was at peace, which revealed David's interest in his own power and military success over his trust in the Lord. God responded to David's sin by punishing all of Israel, which opened David's eyes to the error of his ways and led to his confession of sin and repentance. Throughout David's life we notice a cycle in his relationship with God that makes it look a lot like ours. David moved from a place of worship to sin, then to repentance, then back to worship. Second Samuel ends with David's example of costly sacrifice as a display of his worship toward God. This theme is the heart of Psalm 24, a psalm that acknowledges the power of God—the Author and Finisher of everything.

H

E

A

R

T

DID YOU KNOW?
David purchased the threshing floor of Araunah (2 Sam. 24:18). Before this high place that contained a threshing floor belonged to Araunah, it was called Mount Moriah, the place where Abraham was tested with sacrificing Isaac (Gen. 22:2). This same high place is where Solomon's temple would later be built (2 Chron. 3:1), followed by Herod's temple. Today the Dome of the Rock sits on this same high place.[9]

MEMORY VERSE
Pick one of the memory verse options for this week—Psalm 1:1-6; Psalm 119:9-11—and write the verse.

DAILY CHALLENGE

There are two paths in life—the path of the righteous or the path of the wicked. Make lists of the words in Psalm 1 that describe the life of the righteous and the life of the wicked. What stands out as you compare the lists you made?

DAY 88 | PSALMS 1; 19

MEMORY VERSES: PSALM 1:1-6; PSALM 119:9-11

From the beginning of time, God has been making Himself known. The two primary ways He reveals Himself are through creation and Scripture, both of which testify to God's power and glory. These revelations of God show up repeatedly in the psalms, which individuals and the collective people of God used and still use to worship Him. Psalm 1 sets the course for the book by presenting an important teaching for life in general: Every person must choose the path he or she will follow—either the path of God or the path of self. One leads to abundant life—the other to destruction. The obvious correct choice is to choose the path of God, which means turning from sin and filling your life with Him and His Word. Psalm 19 also echoes the benefit of choosing the right path and responding positively to God's revelation of Himself in creation and His Word. God's ultimate revelation of Himself, which all of Scripture points to, came in Jesus Christ, our Rock and our Redeemer (19:14). When we choose to live in obedience to God and His Word, we are choosing abundant life with Christ.

H

E

A

R

T

DAY 89 | PSALMS 103; 119:1-48

MEMORY VERSES: PSALM 1:1-6; PSALM 119:9-11

In Psalm 103 David praised God because of all the good things He had done, outlining the benefits we receive from Him through His unmerited grace. David noted that the faithful love of God is great and incomparable. God is the ultimate Father in His compassion to His children, and for this He is worthy of our never-ending praise. Psalm 119 picks up some of the same themes from yesterday's readings in Psalms 1 and 19, as the psalmist praised God for His Word and the impact it had on his life. The God who forgives our sins, redeems our lives, and satisfies our desires (103:1-5) is the same God who gives us access into the very heart of who He is through His Word. Because God's Word is such a gift, He expects it to be taken seriously, which means we strive for obedience to God's laws and claim His Word as the compass for our lives. The power, inspiration, and truth of God's Word demand the careful study and dedicated application of it, the end result of which is unspeakable joy (119:23-24).

H

E

A

R

T

READ ON

Psalm 103:12 reveals the powerful truth that God removes our transgressions as far as the east is from the west. Praise God that our sins will not be tossed back in our faces because He has already tossed them behind His back! Take a few minutes to look up the following verses that speak the same truth to us over and over again.

- Isaiah 38:17
- Isaiah 43:25
- Jeremiah 31:34
- Jeremiah 50:20
- Micah 7:19
- Colossians 2:14

MEMORY VERSE

Continue practicing the memory verse you chose. Write out as much of it as you can from memory, and then check to see how you did.

DAY 90 | PSALM 119:49-128

MEMORY VERSES: PSALM 1:1-6; PSALM 119:9-11

WEEK IN REVIEW

Spend some time reflecting on what you have learned this week. Record a truth from each day that you want to remember, or go back and highlight portions of your journal.

DAY 1:

DAY 2:

DAY 3:

DAY 4:

DAY 5:

Psalm 119 is the longest psalm and the longest chapter of the Bible, and almost every verse describes an aspect of God's Word. The verses from today's reading teach us many truths about God and how we are to relate to Him. For example, God's faithful love comes to those who trust Him and brings hope to the afflicted. Reading and studying God's Word is also how people come to know God more deeply, since it is His own revelation of Himself. God's Word is certain and eternal, and the entirety of Scripture reveals the character and glory of God. As we can see from this psalm, God expects His people to know, obey, and delight in His Word. Doing so reveals our faith in and love for Him, and it keeps us on the path toward holiness—a pursuit that will take a lifetime.

H

E

A

R

T

DAY 91 | PSALMS 119:129-176; 139

MEMORY VERSES: PSALM 139:1-3; PSALM 139:15-16

The remainder of Psalm 119 continues the theme of delighting in God's Word. Today's reading reminds us that while God's principles are a joy to obey, many do not follow them. This truth should be a source of sorrow for us as it was for the psalmist, and it should compel us to live on mission for the gospel. Verses 153-159 teach that the way God's people show their love for Him is through obedience to His Word, which challenges us to oppose sin and pursue Christlikeness. Among the promises God makes to His people is the promise that He will help us as we strive to live, study, and obey His Word (119:169-176). This is encouraging no matter where we are in our spiritual journey. The psalm ends with a reminder that the goal of delighting in God's Word is obedience while we wait for our promised eternal life with God to become reality.

H

E

A

R

T

WEEK AT A GLANCE
This week we'll finish reading in Psalms and begin our reading in 1 Kings. At this time in Israel's history, King David was nearing death, which would be followed by the establishment of Solomon's throne and the building of the temple.

DAY 92 | PSALMS 148-150

MEMORY VERSES: PSALM 139:1-3; PSALM 139:15-16

DAILY CHALLENGE

We see in each of these Psalms many reasons to praise the Lord from creation to the creature. Which part of creation causes praise to well up in you? Which part leaves you in awe of its Maker? Draw a picture if you feel inspired, or spend time looking at pictures of God's creation and worshiping the Lord.

The book of Psalms includes 150 individual psalms, hymns of worship to God, with themes that range from praise to lament, and from thanksgiving to songs of ascent (specific psalms used during times of Israelite feasts and religious pilgrimages). The book ends with three psalms of praise. Psalm 148 praises God for His glory, made evident through His creation. The final verse of that psalm references a horn God raised up for His people, which is a reference to the honor God bestows on His people through His redemptive grace. While God did this time and again for His people in the Old Testament, the final and perfect act came when He sent His Son to be our Redeemer. In Psalm 149 the focus remains on praising God, but the emphasis shifts to His acts on behalf of His people and the appropriate way we should respond to Him. Psalm 150 closes the book with shouts of praise and the call for everything that has breath to praise the Lord. These psalms are a great reminder to us that God is always worthy of our praise, and that is the very act for which we were created.

H

E

A

MEMORY VERSE

Pick one of the memory verse options for this week—Psalm 139:1-3; Psalm 139:15-16—and write the verse.

R

T

DAY 93 | 1 KINGS 2

MEMORY VERSES: PSALM 139:1-3; PSALM 139:15-16

The book of 1 Kings picks up where 2 Samuel left off with the transition from David's kingship to that of his son Solomon. Solomon's rise to power wasn't without controversy—Adonijah, his older brother, saw himself as the rightful heir to the throne, and Solomon killed him in order to maintain peace and establish his authority as king. After David made Solomon king and David was about to die, he gave Solomon some parting wisdom. David told Solomon to make obedience to God his primary ambition so that God would continue to be faithful to His covenant promises. Solomon's predecessors—Saul and David—had learned the hard way the importance of obedience to their covenant with God. Both men had made mistakes that Solomon could learn from, but as his story unfolds, it becomes evident that Solomon too was a broken human leader who was unable to faithfully uphold his covenant with God. Thankfully, as God's children today, we are recipients of God's covenant of grace, which means our relationship with God is based on Jesus's perfect obedience rather than our own efforts.

H

E

A

R

T

DAY 94 | 1 KINGS 3; 6

MEMORY VERSES: PSALM 139:1-3; PSALM 139:15-16

THINK ABOUT IT

God has always desired to dwell among His people, which we see evidence of throughout Scripture, from Genesis to Revelation:

- In the garden
- In the tabernacle
- In the temple
- Through Jesus
- Through the Holy Spirit
- In the new Jerusalem

MEMORY VERSE

Continue practicing the memory verse you chose. Write out as much of it as you can from memory, and then check to see how you did.

With the kingship secured, Solomon turned his attention to ruling Israel. Early on, God appeared to Solomon in a dream and gave him the opportunity to ask for anything. Solomon knew that the responsibility he had as God's anointed king would require great wisdom, so that is what he asked for. God granted his request and gave him riches and honor as well. The story in 1 Kings 3:16-28 shows God was faithful to give Solomon the wisdom he asked for. During David's time as king, he had asked God to let him build a temple for Him, but God told him that was not part of His plan for David's rule; instead, that became Solomon's primary task as God's anointed leader. In the midst of Solomon's great success and grand projects, God gave guidance on how to genuinely honor Him. The key to honoring the Lord does not lie primarily in outward expressions of devotion, but in learning and obeying His commands. The temple could crumble (and eventually did), but unselfish dedication and service to God bear fruits that last for eternity.

H

E

A

R

T

DAY 95 | 1 KINGS 8; 9:1-9

MEMORY VERSES: PSALM 139:1-3; PSALM 139:15-16

With the temple and Solomon's own palace complete, Solomon assembled the elders of Israel at Jerusalem. The priests and Levites brought the ark of the Lord and the sacred furnishings from the tabernacle and placed them in the temple. After the Lord's glory in the form of a cloud filled the temple, Solomon offered a prayer of dedication, thanking God for keeping His promise to David, asking God to fulfill the remaining promises He had made to David (2 Sam. 7:5-16), and asking God to hear and answer the Israelites when they prayed in times of need. Then God spoke to Solomon and emphasized the importance of obedience for Israel's continued blessing. The call to obedience surfaces time and again in Scripture, which points to its importance as one of the most important disciplines a follower of God can foster. For Christians today, obedience to God does not earn us salvation—that has been freely given to us through Jesus. Instead, obedience is our loving response to God for who He is and all He has done for us. It's also the primary way we display our devotion to God to a watching world.

H

E

A

R

T

WEEK IN REVIEW
Spend some time reflecting on what you have learned this week. Record a truth from each day that you want to remember, or go back and highlight portions of your journal.

DAY 1:

DAY 2:

DAY 3:

DAY 4:

DAY 5:

DAY 96 | PROVERBS 1–2

MEMORY VERSES: PROVERBS 1:7; PROVERBS 3:5-6

The book of Proverbs and the book of Ecclesiastes are results of Solomon's prayer for wisdom. Proverbs contains some of the most practical advice in the entire Bible, and its wisdom covers everything from relationships to leadership, from how to spend money to how to spend time. Proverbs begins with a prologue stating that the purpose of the book is to provide wisdom and insight for how to live as a child of God. Next, chapters 1–2 describe why a person should desire wisdom and the benefits wisdom brings to a person's life. At its core, wisdom is the skill of living life according to God's ways, which Solomon summarized in Proverbs 1:7: "The fear of the LORD is the beginning of knowledge; fools despise wisdom and discipline." Fear of God speaks to the awe and wonder that results from understanding who God is and how entirely dependent we are on Him. This is the foundation on which everything else in our lives is built.

H

E

A

R

T

WEEK AT A GLANCE
This week we'll be reading mostly in Proverbs. This will be a nice change of pace from the historical book of 1 Kings that we've been reading. Enjoy these very practical bits of godly wisdom.

DAY 97 | PROVERBS 3-4

MEMORY VERSES: PROVERBS 1:7; PROVERBS 3:5-6

Proverbs 3–4 continues Solomon's instructions to those in their youth. In these two chapters, as in other parts of Proverbs, wisdom is personified as a woman seeking others who will listen to her teachings. Whether or not a person listens determines the path of his or her life. Those who fail to heed her instructions will suffer devastating consequences, while those who pursue wisdom will receive many benefits, as these chapters describe. In chapter 4 Solomon roots his plea for wise living in his own upbringing and the tradition of the Israelites—David passed down the importance of wisdom to Solomon, and Solomon passed it on to his children through discipleship. Chapter 3 makes it clear that we gain wisdom through the study of God's Word first and foremost. The Bible is God's revelation of Himself and His truth, and it teaches us how to live for God and share His love with the world. The close of chapter 3 points out an important teaching—one of the reasons we need wisdom for living is so that we know how to relate in godly love to the people in our lives.

H

E

A

R

T

DAILY CHALLENGE

My life verse is Proverbs 4:23—"Guard your heart above all else, for it is the source of life." When I became a believer, the Lord showed me that my heart was always what had gotten me into trouble, so I have to work to guard it unto the Lord. Make a list of ways you can follow the guidance of this proverb.

MEMORY VERSE

Pick one of the memory verse options for this week—Proverbs 1:7; Proverbs 3:5-6—and write the verse.

DAY 98 | PROVERBS 16–18

MEMORY VERSES: PROVERBS 1:7; PROVERBS 3:5-6

THINK ABOUT IT
Of the proverbs you read in Proverbs 16–18, which one stood out to you as the words of wisdom you most needed to hear today? Spend some time with the Lord in prayer, reflecting on the truth He revealed to you.

Proverbs 16–18 are part of a larger division of the book of Proverbs that contains wisdom for everyday life. Three of the most well-known proverbs are found in these chapters: "Pride comes before destruction, and an arrogant spirit before a fall" (Prov. 16:18). "The name of the LORD is a strong tower; the righteous run to it and are protected" (18:10). "One with many friends may be harmed, but there is a friend who stays closer than a brother" (18:24). These three proverbs show the diversity of topics and teachings presented throughout this book. From these proverbs alone, we are reminded that pride is a destructive sin, God is our Protector, and everyone needs the support and love of trusted friends. What these and all other proverbs have in common is that they teach us how to put God's values into practice in our daily lives, which is something we will spend the rest of our lives learning how to do.

H

E

A

R

T

DAY 99 | PROVERBS 31

MEMORY VERSES: PROVERBS 1:7; PROVERBS 3:5-6

Proverbs 31 is known for its description of biblical womanhood, which is why you may have heard someone reference "the Proverbs 31 woman." But this final proverb is about much more than being a woman. Proverbs 31 closes the book with a picture of godly wisdom on display in family life. The virtuous wife and mother described here gives all parents an example to follow as they strive to be husbands, wives, fathers, and mothers who parent, love, and work in godliness. The main principles affirmed in this proverb are a person's trustworthiness, responsibility, and godliness. Whether or not you are a parent, those are characteristics that can only be lived out if you are seeking God's wisdom for daily living. Verse 30 draws attention to the fear of the Lord as an admirable quality, which brings the book of Proverbs full circle from where it began in 1:7. Worship of and respectful submission to the Lord's authority is the key to wisdom in every area of life.

THINK ABOUT IT

Idle time can become idol time. We never want to be lazy or idle in our pursuit of God and in our obedience to Him. This doesn't mean we'll never have downtime or should feel guilty for relaxing. Instead, we're to be on the lookout for patterns of idleness. Do any come to mind? Carefully evaluate if that idleness is holding you back in your walk with the Lord.

MEMORY VERSE

Continue practicing the memory verse you chose. Write out as much of it as you can from memory, and then check to see how you did.

H

E

A

R

T

DAY 100 | 1 KINGS 11–12

MEMORY VERSES: PROVERBS 1:7; PROVERBS 3:5-6

WEEK IN REVIEW

Spend some time reflecting on what you have learned this week. Record a truth from each day that you want to remember, or go back and highlight portions of your journal.

DAY 1:

DAY 2:

DAY 3:

DAY 4:

DAY 5:

First Kings 11 marks a turning point for Solomon and the kingdom of Israel. At this point in his life, Solomon had seven hundred wives and three hundred concubines whom he allowed to practice pagan religions, even constructing places of worship for them. Solomon's life of excessive wisdom and riches (which were originally gifts from God) led him to compromise his faith and his leadership through disobedience, and the consequences were quick and devastating. God judged Solomon by dividing the kingdom of Israel in two. Tensions had been growing among the tribes, and only the grace of God held the kingdom together. Now that it was no more, the kingdom of God's people divided into two. Although Solomon was a wise and godly ruler for much of his life, the end of his reign is yet another reminder of our need for a true and better King, which we have in Jesus. We are also reminded through this story of God's faithfulness to His people—God did not turn His back on either of the kingdoms, and the story of His faithfulness and pursuit of His people continued on toward completion.

H

E

A

R

T

DAY 101 | 1 KINGS 16:29-34; 17

MEMORY VERSES: PSALM 17:15; PSALM 63:1

After the division of the kingdoms, 1 Kings catalogs a long list of kings of Israel and Judah. The evils of the kings of the divided kingdom seem to get progressively worse, climaxing with the rule of King Ahab. Verse 31 of chapter 16 tells us that the sins of previous kings were trivial in comparison to the sins of Ahab, which included his blatant worship of Baal, the building of temples and altars to Baal, and his marriage to Jezebel, a priestess of Baal. As great as Ahab's sins were, the worst part was that he committed these sins while leading a nation, which means he inevitably led all of Israel, the chosen people of God, down the same evil path. No wonder God's anger was provoked. As chapter 17 documents, it was into this perverse national state that the Lord sent His prophet Elijah to proclaim the truth and judgment of God upon His people in a call for their repentance. Even amid some of Israel's darkest days, the Lord sent a light to His people and offered them a way out of the darkness. He has done the same for us today through the light of the gospel.

H

E

A

R

T

WEEK AT A GLANCE
This week we'll continue through 1 Kings as we witness more aftermath of the kingdom being divided. We also get a glimpse into the ministries of two of the great prophets of God: Elijah and Elisha.

DAY 102 | 1 KINGS 18–19

MEMORY VERSES: PSALM 17:15; PSALM 63:1

DAILY CHALLENGE

Make a list of the things you're tempted to believe are more powerful than God. Think about things like your health, family, career, and reputation. Take some time to pray through the idols on your list. Remind yourself of the second commandment—"Do not have other gods besides me" (Ex. 20:3).

MEMORY VERSE

Pick one of the memory verse options for this week—Psalm 17:15; Psalm 63:1—and write the verse.

First Kings 18–19 describe some of the highs and lows of Elijah's ministry. God gave Elijah the responsibility to confront the idolatry in the land, so Elijah assembled Ahab and the prophets of Baal on Mount Carmel for a contest between God and Baal. Identical sacrifices were prepared and the deity who would send fire to consume His sacrifice would show Israel whom to worship. The prophets of Baal tried all day to coax their god to send fire, but nothing happened. After Elijah offered a simple prayer, God responded with fire, causing the people to recognize the power of the one true God. The events on the mountain enraged Jezebel, and she threatened to kill Elijah. He was forced to flee into the wilderness where he thought he would die. From his place of fear and hiding, though, Elijah listened to the quiet voice of the Lord, who reminded him of his calling and encouraged him to continue in his ministry. When we accept Christ as Savior, we still face daily choices of whether to seek and follow the Lord's guidance and to rely on His strength or to seek and rely on our own.

H

E

A

R

T

DAY 103 | 1 KINGS 21-22

MEMORY VERSES: PSALM 17:15; PSALM 63:1

The book of 1 Kings closes with a picture of the full extent of Ahab's evil and the incomparable grace and mercy of God. Ahab desired the vineyard of a man named Naboth, but Naboth refused to sell it to him. As a result, Jezebel devised a plan to accuse Naboth falsely and have him stoned to death. After Naboth's death, Elijah met Ahab and condemned him. The prophet said that the king's family would come to a disastrous end and that he and Jezebel would die violent deaths. That news led Ahab to do something he had never done before— he repented of his sins and humbled himself before God. With that demonstration of repentance, God postponed the family's destruction until after Ahab's death— an action that shows no one is outside of the reach of God's grace and mercy. A few years later Ahab encouraged King Jehoshaphat of Judah to join him in a war, but Jehoshaphat insisted on first hearing from God's prophets. While Jehoshaphat was well-intentioned, neither he nor Ahab listened to God's prophet Micaiah, who warned of defeat, and Ahab died in battle. Micaiah's example reminds us that only in being transformed by faith are we able to understand God's will and receive the strength to stand firm on God's Word in the face of the world's pressures.

DAILY CHALLENGE

God showed Ahab grace when he repented of his sins and humbled himself before God. Write out a prayer of repentance and humility to God. Seek God and listen for His voice.

H

E

A

R

T

DAY 104 | 2 KINGS 2

MEMORY VERSES: PSALM 17:15; PSALM 63:1

MEMORY VERSE

Continue practicing the memory verse you chose. Write out as much of it as you can from memory, and then check to see how you did.

The book of 2 Kings picks up the historical narrative of the Northern and Southern Kingdoms where it left off at the end of 1 Kings. In chapter 2 we read of Elijah's exit from earth by being taken up to heaven in a chariot of fire. After Elijah was gone, the biblical writer focused on Elisha as the Lord's prophet. Various events of miraculous healing and signs from the Lord are described in 2 Kings 2–4 as being performed by Elisha among the people. It is interesting to note how so many of Elisha's miraculous works closely parallel those of Jesus in the Gospels—healings, raising from the dead, feeding thousands, and so on. Elisha's miracles helped the people understand that he was God's prophet and that God had not abandoned His people after He took Elijah away. The Gospels provide us with that same assurance today, as we are reminded of the great lengths God went to demonstrate His love for us and to call us to faith in Him. Even after Jesus ascended to heaven, God sent His Holy Spirit who remains our only source of hope and assurance even today.

H

E

A

R

T

DAY 105 | 2 KINGS 5; 6:1-23

MEMORY VERSES: PSALM 17:15; PSALM 63:1

Second Kings 5 tells the story of Naaman, an Aramean army commander who came to Israel seeking a cure for his skin disease. The Israelite king sent Naaman to Elisha, who in turn sent instructions for Naaman to wash in the Jordan River. It took the persuasion of Naaman's servants to convince him to listen to and trust God's prophet and to follow his instructions. Naaman reminds us that we all are in need of God's healing power because of the way sin wreaks havoc in our lives. As Naaman's example shows, God is ready and willing to cleanse and restore us when we humbly approach Him with our need. After Naaman was healed, he tried to give Elisha a gift, but Elisha refused. The prophet's attendant, Gehazi, privately tried to get something from the commander. Consequently, Gehazi was stricken with a skin disease. The parallel reversal of fortunes that take place in Naaman's and Gehazi's lives remind us that God's power alone transforms us from being selfish and disobedient people to being humble, obedient children of God.

H

E

A

R

T

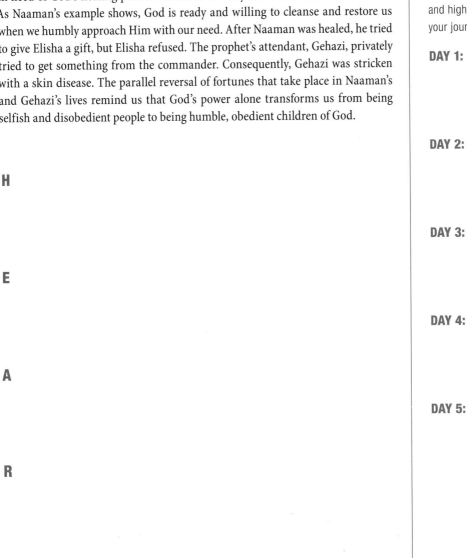

WEEK IN REVIEW
Spend some time reflecting on what you have learned this week. Record a truth from each day that you want to remember, or go back and highlight portions of your journal.

DAY 1:

DAY 2:

DAY 3:

DAY 4:

DAY 5:

DAY 106 | JONAH 1-2

MEMORY VERSES: PSALM 16:11; JOHN 11:25-26

This week's readings shift to the Minor Prophets, short books by God's prophets who had very specific prophecies for God's people. Jonah was one of these prophets, albeit reluctantly. God called Jonah to proclaim His message of judgment on Nineveh, a city in the Assyrian Empire. However, Jonah disobeyed God's call, choosing instead to board a ship going in the opposite direction from Nineveh. Because he fled from God, the Lord sent a violent storm that brought Jonah face to face with his sin and a large fish. One of the running themes throughout the book of Jonah is God's salvation. In chapter 1 the sailors were physically saved when God stopped the storm after Jonah's confession, and in chapter 2 Jonah also was physically saved by God. These physical salvations set the stage for the spiritual salvation through repentance that was at the heart of Jonah's message to the Ninevites. God offers all people today spiritual salvation through the sacrificial work of Jesus who died on the cross to save us from our sins. Once we accept God's offer of salvation, we become His messengers like Jonah was, tasked with sharing that same good news of the gospel with others.

H

WEEK AT A GLANCE

This week we'll read from four of the Minor Prophets—Jonah, Hosea, Amos, and Joel. Some of these prophets were contemporaries of each other, meaning they lived and prophesied during the same time frame. As you read, look for similarities and differences in their prophetic messages to the people of God.

E

A

R

T

DAY 107 | JONAH 3-4

MEMORY VERSES: PSALM 16:11; JOHN 11:25-26

After the fish spit Jonah out alive, God repeated His command for the prophet to go to Nineveh and deliver a message to its people. This time Jonah did not hesitate to obey. He warned the Ninevites of God's judgment against their sins, and the people responded by believing in God and repenting. Even the king repented and ordered the people to fast, pray, and change their sinful ways. However, Jonah's heart for the Ninevites had not changed from his initial refusal to go, and he was furious that God saved this nation. While Jonah waited to see what God would do with the people, God used a shade plant to teach His prophet an important lesson about divine compassion. Jonah's story reminds us how important it is that we have hearts aligned with God's. God has made us His ambassadors to a dying world, which means we have to open our eyes to the countless people around us who desperately need the grace of God. As we mimic God's compassion, He will increase our hearts for the lost and draw us closer to Himself.

DAILY CHALLENGE

Spend a few minutes making a list of the people in your life who need to realize and place faith in God's grace. Make these people a focus of your prayers as you brainstorm ways to share the gospel.

H

E

A

R

T

MEMORY VERSE

Pick one of the memory verse options for this week—Psalm 16:11; John 11:25-26—and write the verse.

DAY 108 | HOSEA 1–3

MEMORY VERSES: PSALM 16:11; JOHN 11:25-26

READ ON

What does it mean to you to call Jesus your Bridegroom? How does this imagery help you better understand your relationship with Him? Read the following passages as you ponder these questions:

- John 3:27-30
- Ephesians 5:22-33
- Revelation 19:6-9
- Revelation 22:6-21

Hosea was another of God's Old Testament prophets who was given a challenging task in order to communicate God's judgment and mercy to the people of Israel. To paint an incredibly symbolic picture, God commanded Hosea to marry a prostitute named Gomer as a representation of Israel's unfaithfulness to God. Hosea did as God told him, and the couple had three children who were each given a name that expressed a divine judgment against Israel. Besides judgment for sin, God also promised restoration—an important reminder of His faithfulness to His people despite their unfaithfulness to Him. Through Hosea God promised that He would not give up on His people. Just as Hosea continually pursued Gomer through her unfaithfulness, God does the same for His people even today. God does more than pursue us, though; He redeems us with His love. As a symbol of God's redemptive love for Israel, He ordered Hosea to redeem and restore Gomer. Hosea's redemption of Gomer foreshadowed Jesus's redemption of us. On the cross Jesus our Bridegroom made a way for us to experience forgiveness and redemption of our sins.

H

E

A

R

T

DAY 109 | AMOS 1:1; 9

MEMORY VERSES: PSALM 16:11; JOHN 11:25-26

Each of God's Old Testament prophets had a specific purpose and focus for their ministry, and for Amos, that calling centered on the rampant idolatry and injustice in the Israelite community. From Amos 1:1 we learn that Amos was not a prophet by trade—he was a sheep breeder. Regardless, God used Amos to point out how far God's people had strayed from Him. Chapter 9 includes God's message of judgment against the people for their sins, but it also includes His message of hope. God, in His justice, had to punish the people for their sins, but He also promised that after the time of judgment, He would restore and repair the broken nation out of faithfulness to His covenant promises. God promised that David's "fallen shelter" (Amos 9:11) would be restored—a promise that was ultimately fulfilled in Jesus, the Messiah, who descended from David's earthly line and brought about the justice and redemption the people needed desperately. Today we also place our hope in Christ for restoration and redemption. Through Christ, God calls us to repentance, just as He did the Israelites. He also calls us to stand up for the injustices in our world as Amos did.

H

E

A

R

T

DAILY CHALLENGE
One of the themes of Amos is the responsibility God's people have to fight back against the injustices in our world. Name one injustice you've witnessed recently and identify a way you can imitate God's compassion and justice in response.

MEMORY VERSE
Continue practicing the memory verse you chose. Write out as much of it as you can from memory, and then check to see how you did.

DAY 110 | JOEL 1–3

MEMORY VERSES: PSALM 16:11; JOHN 11:25-26

WEEK IN REVIEW

Spend some time reflecting on what you have learned this week. Record a truth from each day that you want to remember, or go back and highlight portions of your journal.

DAY 1:

DAY 2:

DAY 3:

DAY 4:

DAY 5:

A common theme throughout the Minor Prophets is that God judges sin and calls His people to repentance. During Joel's day, a severe locust plague overtook Judah, an event that Joel understood to be a sign of God's looming judgment against the people for their lack of concern and conviction over sin. But God, out of compassion for His people, sent the plague as well as a prophecy of a coming invasion to draw His people back to Himself. Again we see God's mercy on display when He promised to restore anyone who repented of his or her sins. God also promised His Holy Spirit who would serve as a sign of His mercy and relationship with them. The apostle Peter quoted Joel 2:28-32 during his Pentecost sermon to assure the people that God was faithful to fulfill the promise He had made (Acts 2:16-21). The book of Joel reminds us of God's power and justice, two of His perfect attributes that are constantly at work in our lives. When we reflect on these traits, we are reminded of the grace God has shown us and should be brought to awe that He has chosen sinful humans like us to be His beloved children.

H

E

A

R

T

DAY 111 | ISAIAH 6; 9

MEMORY VERSES: ISAIAH 53:5-6; 1 PETER 2:23-24

The heart of the book of Isaiah is to demonstrate God's holiness and grace and issue a call for His people to return to Him in obedience and faith. Isaiah 6 records Isaiah's encounter with God when he was called to be a prophet. Isaiah's response to God's commission—"Here I am. Send me." (Isa. 6:8)—is one of the greatest pictures of obedience in all of Scripture. In Isaiah 9 we read the first of many Messianic prophecies in the book when God promised the birth of a child who would deliver His people. Matthew revealed in his Gospel that Isaiah's prophecy pointed to the birth of Jesus, the One who takes away the sins of the world. Despite our disobedience and sinfulness, God has given us a Redeemer in Jesus, and through Him, we gain eternal life in the presence of that same glorious God Isaiah witnessed.

H

E

A

R

T

WEEK AT A GLANCE
We'll spend most of this week reading sections from one of the Major Prophets, Isaiah. The authors of the New Testament quoted or alluded to Isaiah more than any other Old Testament book (although Psalms is a very close second), because it talks so often about the coming of the Messiah, whom we know to be Jesus. We'll finish this week by reading Micah, a prophet whose ministry overlapped with Isaiah's.

DAY 112 | ISAIAH 44–45

MEMORY VERSES: ISAIAH 53:5-6; 1 PETER 2:23-24

THINK ABOUT IT

Spend some extra time in prayer today reflecting on God as your Creator and Sustainer and praising Him for His work in and through you.

While the first half of Isaiah is about God's judgment for people's sins, the second half brings words of peace and hope to the people as He reminds them of His covenant by continuing to point them to the coming Messiah. In today's reading, God reminded the people that He chose them, and that He alone—not any of their man-made idols—has the power to restore them. With powerful imagery, God listed many ways that the people's idols were foolish and helpless to save them. Isaiah also prophesied about how King Cyrus of Persia would defeat the Babylonians and help bring God's people back from exile. These chapters remind us that God alone is the Creator and Sustainer of the world and that He orchestrates everything according to His will and good purposes. When life seems hopeless and God seems far away, God's faithfulness to His people throughout Scripture reminds us that He is always at work in our lives.

H

E

MEMORY VERSE

Pick one of the memory verse options for this week—Isaiah 53:5-6; 1 Peter 2:23-24—and write the verse.

A

R

T

DAY 113 | ISAIAH 52-53

MEMORY VERSES: ISAIAH 53:5-6; 1 PETER 2:23-24

Isaiah 52–53 is part of Isaiah's Servant Song, a lengthy prophecy about Jesus, the Messiah and Suffering Servant of God. In these chapters we read about God's solution for His people's sin problem: God would send His servant to suffer on humanity's behalf, an act that would bear the punishment for all human sin and extend forgiveness to all who would believe. Unlike the Israelites, who continued to fall into patterns of disobedience and lack of faith, the coming Servant would be obedient and faithful always, even at the cost of His own life. As people living on this side of the cross, we know that only Jesus, the Son of God, could live the perfect and sinless life necessary to be the sacrifice for our sins. When we reflect on the suffering Jesus endured and the lengths God went to in order to offer us forgiveness and eternal life in Him, we can't help but want to live our lives in service to Him.

DID YOU KNOW?
Jesus referred to Himself as Isaiah's Suffering Servant in Luke 22:37, when He quoted Isaiah 53:12, "For I tell you, what is written must be fulfilled in me: *And he was counted among the lawless.* Yes, what is written about me is coming to its fulfillment."

H

E

A

R

T

DAY 114 | ISAIAH 65–66

MEMORY VERSES: ISAIAH 53:5-6; 1 PETER 2:23-24

DID YOU KNOW?

The main theme of the book of Isaiah is the one true God—His holiness and relationship to the people and world He created.

MEMORY VERSE

Continue practicing the memory verse you chose. Write out as much of it as you can from memory, and then check to see how you did.

Through God's use of Isaiah, the Israelites were convicted of their sins, recognized God's faithful love, and prayed for Him to again look with favor upon them (Isa. 63–64). The book closes with God's response to Israel's prayer, which was a final reminder of His faithful love and their repeated disobedience. God used Isaiah to tell the people that they would be punished for their sins but that they would also be restored to Him, and eventually, that restoration would be eternal. As a result, people everywhere would recognize God for who He is and serve and worship Him in response. From the vision of the future in Revelation, we are reminded that one day this eternal worship will be a reality for all of God's people. And so in the meantime we are to serve God and live for Him today.

H

E

A

R

T

DAY 115 | MICAH 1; 4:6-13; 5

MEMORY VERSES: ISAIAH 53:5-6; 1 PETER 2:23-24

The prophet Micah's ministry overlapped with Isaiah's and shared many of the same themes, but Micah targeted his prophecies at the Southern Kingdom, Judah. Like Isaiah, Micah's prophecies describe God's judgment of wickedness and His mercy for those who come to Him in repentance and faith. The main sin God spoke out against was idolatry. These were God's people, but they rejected Him and His laws by allowing and even participating in idol worship. As we saw in Isaiah, though, Micah also prophesied about the hope that would come through a Deliverer. Micah proclaims a few different Messianic prophecies about Jesus, including His birth in Bethlehem, His second coming, and eternal reign. Some of these promises have already come to pass. However, we can have confidence in God today, knowing that He will be faithful to do what He has promised. The promised return of Jesus gives us the hope and strength we need to face all of life's present difficulties, and it should motivate us to live in daily obedience to Him.

H

E

A

R

T

WEEK IN REVIEW
Spend some time reflecting on what you have learned this week. Record a truth from each day that you want to remember, or go back and highlight portions of your journal.

DAY 1:

DAY 2:

DAY 3:

DAY 4:

DAY 5:

DAY 116 | 2 KINGS 17-18

MEMORY VERSES: PROVERBS 29:18; JEREMIAH 1:15

In Genesis God made a covenant with Abraham that He reiterated to Isaac and Jacob, and that promise included plans for a specific portion of land where God's people would live. However, today's reading in 2 Kings reveals that because of the people's cyclical pattern of disobedience they lost inheritance of the promised land. Through countless judges, prophets, and other leaders, God repeatedly warned the people to turn back to Him, but they abandoned His invitation, causing God to allow them to be taken captive by the Assyrians and forced into another exile. At the same time, King Hezekiah attempted to reform the southern kingdom of Judah by leading the people back to God. These chapters remind us that God's judgment is serious, but it is never without just cause: God had shown His people incredible grace, but they refused to turn to Him. Furthermore, Hezekiah is a reminder for us that no matter how tempted or pressured we may feel to turn our backs on God, we can always trust in His goodness and sovereignty over our lives.

H

E

A

R

T

WEEK AT A GLANCE

This week we'll be reading about the Assyrian captivity due to Israel's continued disobedience. Hezekiah was the king of Judah at that time, and he prayed to God for deliverance, which God provided. Through our reading, we'll see the rise of a few more kings and the call of the prophet Jeremiah.

DAY 117 | 2 KINGS 19–21

MEMORY VERSES: PROVERBS 29:18; JEREMIAH 1:15

Hezekiah was a man of God, as evidenced through his prayers. Hezekiah prayed to God for deliverance from Assyria, and God delivered the city. Later, when Hezekiah was suffering from a terminal illness, he prayed for God to remember his faithfulness, and God added fifteen more years to his life. However, Hezekiah wasn't perfect, and when he acted prideful over his treasures (which were blessings from God that Hezekiah took for granted), the prophet Isaiah warned him that eventually Judah would experience a fate like Israel's, and all his treasures would be gone. After Hezekiah died, the nation was ruled by two of its most wicked kings to date. God warned that His judgment was pending. While God's grace and patience for His people is limitless, we all come to a place where we must face the consequences of our sins. In those moments, it is crucial to remember that God never withholds His love and grace from us. We are the ones who have drifted from Him.

DAILY CHALLENGE

After reading Hezekiah's prayer in 2 Kings 19:14-19, write your own prayer to the Lord reflecting on what He has revealed to you today.

MEMORY VERSE

Pick one of the memory verse options for this week—Proverbs 29:18; Jeremiah 1:15—and write the verse.

H

E

A

R

T

DAY 118 | 2 KINGS 22–23

MEMORY VERSES: PROVERBS 29:18; JEREMIAH 1:15

DID YOU KNOW?

God's Word tells us King Josiah "did what was right in the LORD's sight and walked in all the ways of his ancestor David; he did not turn to the right or the left" (2 Kings 22:2). We also read, "Before him there was no king like him who turned to the LORD with all his heart and with all his soul and with all his strength according to all the law of Moses, and no one like him arose after him" (23:25). Josiah models for us a life of faithfulness and obedience to God.

King Josiah stood in sharp contrast to his father Amon and his grandfather Manasseh, and as a result, significant cultural changes began to take place during Josiah's reign. While God's temple was being repaired, the books of Law—Genesis to Deuteronomy—was discovered, and upon hearing it read, Josiah realized the nation was guilty of breaking the covenant and in danger of divine wrath. God's Word has always had the power to bring sin to light and turn hardened hearts toward repentance. Josiah renewed the covenant before the people and initiated a spiritual reform movement that rid the nation of idolatry and renewed times of worship and celebration before God. While these were all positive changes, Josiah was the last righteous king of Judah. His death paved the way for the judgment against sin that God's prophets had warned against. Josiah's example reminds us that our obedience to God is rooted in our relationship with Him and our acceptance of the authority of His Word in our lives.

H

E

A

R

T

DAY 119 | JEREMIAH 1–3:5

MEMORY VERSES: PROVERBS 29:18; JEREMIAH 1:15

Jeremiah became God's prophet during the reign of King Josiah and remained a prophet through the last of Judah's kings. This was a tumultuous time in the nation's history, and God had stern warnings He wanted His people to hear through His prophet. It is no surprise that Jeremiah was hesitant to obey God's calling. Jeremiah tried to avoid God's call with various excuses, but God revealed to the prophet that He had chosen him before birth for this very task. Idolatry— a violation of the first and second commandments—was again revealed as the major sin the people were guilty of, which in turn created a rift in their relationship with God. Through Jeremiah, God offered the people yet another chance for repentance, but He also warned of the judgment that was coming. Like Jeremiah, our task as God's representatives today is to listen to His Word, obey His call, and share the truth of His love and the need for repentance with others.

H

E

A

R

T

DAILY CHALLENGE

Like many of the prophets we read about in the Bible, Jeremiah was hesitant to deliver God's challenging message, and he tried to use his young age as an excuse to avoid his calling. What excuses have you used lately to avoid serving God in a particular way? How does Jeremiah's encounter with God speak into that situation?

MEMORY VERSE

Continue practicing the memory verse you chose. Write out as much of it as you can from memory, and then check to see how you did.

DAY 120 | JEREMIAH 25; 29

MEMORY VERSES: PROVERBS 29:18; JEREMIAH 1:15

WEEK IN REVIEW

Spend some time reflecting on what you have learned this week. Record a truth from each day that you want to remember, or go back and highlight portions of your journal.

DAY 1:

DAY 2:

DAY 3:

DAY 4:

DAY 5:

For twenty-three years Jeremiah delivered the same call of repentance to the people of Judah time and time again, but the people refused to listen to him. Unfortunately, the time for God's judgment had come, and Jeremiah told them that the nation was about to be overpowered by the Babylonians. Jeremiah described a cup of God's wrath that all the wicked nations would drink as punishment from God, imagery that brings to mind Jesus's prayer in the garden of Gethsemane prior to His crucifixion: "My Father, if it is possible, let this cup pass from me. Yet not as I will, but as you will" (Matt. 26:39). By going to the cross, Jesus drank the cup of God's wrath, taking all sin of humankind on Himself in order to satisfy God's divine justice. In Jeremiah 29 we also read that God used the prophet to provide hope to some of the people of Judah who had been taken into exile in Babylon. Jeremiah sent a letter to them, encouraging them to make the best of their situation because the exile would last for seventy years. Jeremiah warned the exiles not to listen to false promises and to find their hope instead in the Lord.

H

E

A

R

T

DAY 121 | JEREMIAH 31:31-40; 32-33

MEMORY VERSES: EZEKIEL 36:26-27; DANIEL 4:35

The first part of Jeremiah contains prophecies about God's judgment against the people of Judah for their sins, but as Jeremiah's prophecies continue, the predictions shift to promises of God's restoration and hope. Because God's love for the people was unending, He planned to establish a new covenant with His people—one based on the transformation of their hearts rather than on laws engraved on stone tablets. The Lord would be with His people, and they would truly know Him. Chapters 32–33 record various promises the Lord made concerning His restored people. He would give them a blessed and hopeful future. Nothing would be too difficult for the Lord to accomplish on their behalf. He would establish an unbreakable covenant with them in the future. God's promised new covenant is a reality for all Christians today, and it is based on the sacrificial blood of Jesus who made a way for us to have our own personal relationships with God and the indwelling presence of the Holy Spirit in our lives.

H

E

A

R

T

WEEK AT A GLANCE
Captivity is on the horizon for the nation of Judah. Our readings in Jeremiah, 2 Kings, Ezekiel, and Daniel will show this come to fruition and its immediate aftermath for God's people. But we'll also be reminded through these same texts that God never leaves His children without hope.

DAY 122 | JEREMIAH 52; 2 KINGS 24–25

MEMORY VERSES: EZEKIEL 36:26-27; DANIEL 4:35

THINK ABOUT IT

When the Israelites were in the wilderness after the exodus, God spent a good deal of time teaching them about the blessings that come from obedience to Him. He also warned them about the consequences of disobedience: "I will scatter you among the nations" (Lev. 26:33). After centuries of disobedience, God did just that (Jer. 52:3). Our God is faithful to His word. What evidence of God's faithfulness have you seen lately?

MEMORY VERSE

Pick one of the memory verse options for this week—Ezekiel 36:26-27; Daniel 4:35—and write the verse.

Jeremiah's prophecies had predicted the fall of Jerusalem as God brought forth His judgment on the people. The book of Jeremiah ends with a narrative of those events, which are also told in 2 Kings 24–25. Three months after Jehoiachin became king, the king of Babylon (Nebuchadnezzar) invaded Judah, took captive the king and his family as well as thousands of leading citizens, and installed Zedekiah, Jehoiachin's relative, as a puppet ruler. Thirty-seven years after being taken captive to Babylon, King Jehoiachin received a pardon from Evil-merodach, the new Babylonian ruler. Jehoiachin's life changed for the better, although he remained a king-in-exile for the rest of his life. Jehoiachin's release signaled the hope of restoration for Judah. God finally held the people of Judah accountable for their centuries of sin and rebellion against Him, but unlike His unfaithful people, God proved even in judgment that He was still faithful and that in Him we find restoration and hope.

H

E

A

R

T

DAY 123 | EZEKIEL 1:1-3; 36:16-38; 37

MEMORY VERSES: EZEKIEL 36:26-27; DANIEL 4:35

With the fall of Jerusalem, the people of Judah were exiled to Babylon. The prophet Ezekiel delivered God's messages to His people while they were in exile, and he was an exile himself. At the heart of Ezekiel's prophecy is God's deliverance and restoration of His people (Ezek. 36:24-26). That God preserved a remnant of exiles from the Northern and Southern Kingdoms reminds us that He never allowed His people to be completely destroyed. Restoration was the imagery behind Ezekiel's vision of the valley of dry bones in chapter 37. Instead of decomposition, God composes. Instead of decay, God restores. Through the power and truth of the Word of God and the presence of the Holy Spirit, you and I are becoming more alive each day, much like these dry bones. When we become Christians, God raises us from spiritual death. As our old nature is dying, our new nature is growing, and God is putting His words in our mouths so we can offer a message of hope and life within a world of death and decay.

DAILY CHALLENGE

The most famous imagery in the book of Ezekiel is the prophet's vision of the valley of dry bones. Draw a picture or write a poem based on your reading of Ezekiel 37 and the picture of life from death it describes.

H

E

A

R

T

DAY 124 | DANIEL 1–2

MEMORY VERSES: EZEKIEL 36:26-27; DANIEL 4:35

DAILY CHALLENGE

Read aloud Daniel's prayer of praise in Daniel 2:19-23.
Then using his prayer as a guide, write your own prayer of praise to God for a recent answered prayer.

Daniel was another of God's prophets who ministered during the exile in Babylon. The Babylonians employed a process of assimilation whereby captive young people were trained to serve in the king's court. Daniel was one of these young men, but the actions he took in Daniel 1–2 show he had no plan to assimilate into Babylonian faith. Daniel and his three friends disciplined themselves to eat only vegetables and drink water so as not to compromise their faithfulness to God in the matter of dietary laws. God gave the faithful young men knowledge, understanding, and wisdom, enabling them to serve wisely for many years. The dream Daniel interpreted in Daniel 2 focused on kingdoms: the power of Nebuchadnezzar's kingdom and a future greater kingdom that would never end. Daniel's interpretation was looking to Jesus Christ, who would institute a new kingdom and whose reign would never end. From the beginning of this prophetic book, we see that God's people can trust in God's power and control along with the goodness of His Word.

H

E

MEMORY VERSE

Continue practicing the memory verse you chose. Write out as much of it as you can from memory, and then check to see how you did.

A

R

T

DAY 125 | DANIEL 3-4

MEMORY VERSES: EZEKIEL 36:26-27; DANIEL 4:35

Daniel 3 records the popular event of three Jewish men—Shadrach, Meshach, and Abednego—who refused to compromise their faith in God. Nebuchadnezzar made a huge statue and demanded that all his subjects bow down and worship it. To refuse to worship the statue meant disobeying the king's decree, which was considered paramount to disobeying the king himself. The failure of the men to bow down to the gold statue was motivated by their own faith relationship with the one true God. In the heat of the king's anger, he ordered the men to be thrown into a furnace of fire, but when the men were thrown into the fire, nothing went as planned. Nebuchadnezzar witnessed firsthand God's presence with His servants in the fiery furnace, and the men emerged unscathed. In chapter 4 the very authority that he attempted to overrule humbles Nebuchadnezzar. As a result, a pagan king was forced to bow down to the holy God. We are reminded that God is present with His people in every threatening situation and uses their faithfulness to glorify His name. Also, we are warned against claiming authority that doesn't belong to us.

WEEK IN REVIEW

Spend some time reflecting on what you have learned this week. Record a truth from each day that you want to remember, or go back and highlight portions of your journal.

DAY 1:

DAY 2:

DAY 3:

DAY 4:

DAY 5:

H

E

A

R

T

DAY 126 | DANIEL 5-6

MEMORY VERSES: DANIEL 6:26-27; DANIEL 9:19

Daniel 5 begins with a feast thrown by King Belshazzar. When Belshazzar saw a vision of a cryptic message written on the wall, God used Daniel to interpret the vision and point out Belshazzar's failure to honor the one true God. Because of the interpretive powers Daniel displayed, he was singled out by officials in the court who felt threatened by him, and these men watched Daniel's life for an opportunity to pit him against the king. Knowing Daniel's faith in God, they manipulated the king to sign into law a mandate that forced everyone to pray only to the king, with the punishment of disobedience being death in a lion's den. Daniel courageously maintained his discipline of prayer even though doing so brought a death sentence in the lions' den. When the king found Daniel alive the next morning, he worshiped God and cast the "wise men" to the lions. As we practice the discipline of prayer, we will grow in our faith in God, trusting that He can help us face any situation with courage. Do not give up on prayer. Prayer will prove to be a lifeline of communication with God.

H

WEEK AT A GLANCE

The Israelites remained in captivity and faced challenge after challenge. As you make your way through your readings, notice how the courage of a few to stand for God and His Word revealed God's power and glory to the leaders of their day.

E

A

R

T

DAY 127 | DANIEL 9–10; 12

MEMORY VERSES: DANIEL 6:26-27; DANIEL 9:19

In addition to demonstrating a life of faithfulness to God through strenuous circumstances, the book of Daniel also includes several chapters of prophecy concerning end-times events. As these prophetic visions of judgment and tribulation unfolded, Daniel prayed for God's forgiveness, repeatedly confessing the sins of the people before Him (Dan. 9). Among the specific things God revealed to Daniel was a time of international turmoil that resulted in the persecution and death of some of His people. There is hope, though, and the time of conflict in persecution will come to an end with the vindication of the righteous. Eternal life awaits those whose names are found written in the book of life, but eternal shame for those who rebelled against God. This eternal life—secured for us through the sacrificial life, death, and resurrection of Jesus—is the source of ultimate hope and confidence for every believer of Christ. We know that Jesus will come again and make eternal life in the presence of God our eternal reality, and until then, we are to live out our mission of being His disciples in a lost and hopeless world.

DAILY CHALLENGE

Where is your greatest hope invested? Is it in a job? In a relationship? Spend some extra time in prayer today. Ask the Spirit to show you where you are placing your hope and to lead you to hope in Christ above all things.

H

E

A

R

T

MEMORY VERSE

Pick one of the memory verse options for this week—Daniel 6:26-27; Daniel 9:19—and write the verse.

DAY 128 | EZRA 1-2

MEMORY VERSES: DANIEL 6:26-27; DANIEL 9:19

DAILY CHALLENGE

God promised to scatter His people for their disobedience to Him, but He also promised to bring them back home (Ezek. 11:14-20). Make a list of the things you would like to see God restore or make whole again in your life. Incorporate these into your daily prayers.

Just as God brought destruction upon the city of Jerusalem through the destruction of the temple of the Lord, so He brought about the eventual restoration of the temple and the return of the exiles as recorded in Ezra. For the first period of the Israelites' return to the city, the Lord spoke to Cyrus, the king of Persia, who also happened to be a Gentile nonbeliever. It was through Cyrus that the Lord made the return of His people possible. Cyrus offered reentry into the land to anyone who would help rebuild the temple, to which he was also going to restore all of the treasures stolen from the original temple by Nebuchadnezzar. The Lord's divine plan is evident through both the exile and return of the people to Jerusalem. This is especially evident in His use of Cyrus to be an instrument for His divine will. Even a Persian king recognized the power, control, and sovereignty of the God of the universe. Like the Jews who responded to the opportunity, we should respond with joy, gratitude, and determination to the opportunities God gives us to be a part of His work also.

H

E

A

R

T

DAY 129 | EZRA 3-4

MEMORY VERSES: DANIEL 6:26-27; DANIEL 9:19

Just months after leaving Babylon, the exiles had rebuilt the altar and restored the formal forms of worship given through Moses. They also hired laborers and purchased building materials so the temple could be rebuilt. The Lord's help was evident in laying the temple's foundation, and they used that as an opportunity for worship and to bring glory to His name. The Jews praised God by declaring His essential character. Their joy came because they seized the opportunity God gave to participate in His work. But credit for the work's success was due to God, not the people. Soon after the exiles arrived in Jerusalem, word of their endeavor reached people living near the ruined city, and opposition to the rebuilding efforts quickly arose. People approached Zerubbabel with an offer of help, but in reality, they opposed the Jewish effort and intended to sabotage it. This opposition brought construction to a standstill, and nothing proceeded for well over a decade. Despite our faithfulness to God, we are guaranteed opposition to His work in the world. As this part of God's story reminds us, opposition can't hinder God's faithfulness to His people or His purposes.

H

E

A

R

T

MEMORY VERSE
Continue practicing the memory verse you chose. Write out as much of it as you can from memory, and then check to see how you did.

DAY 130 | EZRA 5-6

MEMORY VERSES: DANIEL 6:26-27; DANIEL 9:19

WEEK IN REVIEW

Spend some time reflecting on what you have learned this week. Record a truth from each day that you want to remember, or go back and highlight portions of your journal.

DAY 1:

DAY 2:

DAY 3:

DAY 4:

DAY 5:

Finally, after more than a decade, construction resumed on the temple. The building activity in Jerusalem raised suspicion among local Persian officials. They allowed the work to continue while they investigated. Discovery of Cyrus's decree insured the completion of the temple. When restoration of the temple was complete, the people participated in Passover, which marked the renewal of religious life for the Jews, who could once again worship in obedience to God's Word. The restored exiles had many reasons for being joyful. Primarily, the Lord made them joyful because the Persian king's attitude had changed. We too should rejoice in a God who directs the decrees of human kings. Since the time of the garden of Eden when sin entered the world, God has been about the business of restoring His people to Himself, and He continues to do so today. At the heart of our restoration is repentance of sin and obedience to Him.

H

E

A

R

T

DAY 131 | ZECHARIAH 1:1-6; 2; 12

MEMORY VERSES: ZEPHANIAH 3:17; 1 PETER 3:15

Zechariah was one of God's prophets appointed to deliver His messages to the Jews who returned to Jerusalem after the exile. One of the reasons God sent Zechariah at this time was to encourage the people to continue their work on the temple even in the face of opposition. Through a series of eight night visions to Zechariah, God revealed His purposes to His people. He would restore their city and their relationship with Him, and eventually, He would give Israel final victory over its enemies. These verses also contain God's promise of a Messiah and His promise to pour out the Spirit of grace and prayer on the people of Jerusalem. These prophecies point ahead to Jesus—the One who was pierced on the cross for the sins of mankind, and the One through whom final victory against sin and death is accomplished. Zechariah also prophesied regarding the coming of the Holy Spirit, which took place after Jesus's resurrection and ascension. As believers, we can rejoice that salvation in Christ brings peace today and hope for eternal peace tomorrow. Salvation is made possible through the suffering of the Messiah.

H

E

A

R

T

WEEK AT A GLANCE
We'll continue reading about the return of the exiles this week. The book of Esther is also in our reading, and it is such a great book! Did you realize you're halfway through your reading plan today? Praise the Lord for your endurance, and let me encourage you to keep up the good work. God still has so much to say to you through His Word.

WEEK 27 | DAY 131 | ZECHARIAH 1:1-6; 2; 12   141

KEY WORD: EZRA

The book of Ezra is named for the man Ezra, a scribe and priest who led a group of exiles back to Jerusalem from Babylon. His name means "help" or "helper," and that is very much the role God gave him among God's people.[11]

MEMORY VERSE

Pick one of the memory verse options for this week—Zephaniah 3:17; 1 Peter 3:15—and write the verse.

DAY 132 | EZRA 7-8

MEMORY VERSES: ZEPHANIAH 3:17; 1 PETER 3:15

Ezra 7–8 tells about the return to Jerusalem for the second group of exiles from Babylon, this time led by Ezra himself. Ezra was a scribe who lived as an exile in the area of Babylon, and he longed to see his homeland again. A new Persian king, Artaxerxes I, finally gave Ezra permission to lead a delegation of exiles back home. Their task was to reestablish proper worship of the God of heaven. God's providential hand appears in every act leading to the return of His people and the restoration of the nation. God not only used faithful believers like Ezra, but also moved pagan rulers like Artaxerxes to participate in His plan. Ezra wanted to implement a spiritual revival in Israel based on God's Word. God's people were meant to lead the way in demonstrating what life can be like when lived in accordance with God and His Word. Today we have the opportunity to obey God and to show a lost world how abundant life can be through faith in Jesus Christ and faithfulness to God's Word.

H

E

A

R

T

DAY 133 | EZRA 9–10

MEMORY VERSES: ZEPHANIAH 3:17; 1 PETER 3:15

After settling into Jerusalem, Ezra received an official report on affairs in Judah, but what Ezra heard was devastating. Instead of living as God's chosen and set apart people, men had married foreign wives, which was a direct opposition to God's covenant. This issue was not one of race or nationalism; it was a spiritual problem because the women worshiped false gods. Casual acceptance of these religions by husbands denied the Lord's claim that He alone was God. Consequently, the nation the Lord commanded to be holy had become no different from its pagan neighbors. Ezra grieved over how far God's people had fallen, and his very public grief moved many people to confession of sins and repentance. As a result, they renewed their covenant with God. Like Ezra, we need to be people who are grieved over the presence of sin in our lives and the lives of our loved ones. God has chosen us and set us apart for His glory to be lights for Him in our world. Only with a healthy view of our sin can we live the life of repentance and obedience to God that He calls us to live for our own good and His glory.

H

E

A

R

T

DAY 134 | ESTHER 1-2

MEMORY VERSES: ZEPHANIAH 3:17; 1 PETER 3:15

DID YOU KNOW?

Esther is one of only two Bible books named for women (Ruth is the other). The book is unusual in that in the original version no name, title, or pronoun for God appears in it. But God's presence is clear throughout the book.[12]

MEMORY VERSE

Continue practicing the memory verse you chose. Write out as much of it as you can from memory, and then check to see how you did.

The events described in the book of Esther cover a ten-year period during the reign of Xerxes I, also known as Ahasuerus. Ahasuerus was an arrogant ruler, and when his queen refused to put herself on display at a lavish and drunken banquet, the king deposed her and launched an empire-wide search for a replacement. The quest for a new queen lasted four years. Esther was brought before Ahasuerus as part of this search. The king loved Esther—she won his favor and was selected as his new queen. Esther's unusual story is a part of Scripture and matters to us today because it is a clear picture of God's providential protection and care of His covenant people. Esther was a Jew whom God placed in a position to influence the destiny of His people and nations at a time when they would need an advocate. Even in our most trying situations, God is always at work for our long-term good, even if in the short term it is not clear how He's doing so. He wants His people to trust Him wholeheartedly and confidently—even in the midst of radical, unexpected change.

H

E

A

R

T

DAY 135 | ESTHER 3-4

MEMORY VERSES: ZEPHANIAH 3:17; 1 PETER 3:15

The plot of the book of Esther thickens in chapter 3 with the introduction of the villain, a man named Haman who had a powerful position in the king's court. Haman descended from a Canaanite tribe who consistently opposed Israel, from the exodus out of Egypt to the reign of David. When Mordecai failed to show Haman the respect he desired, he determined to eliminate all the Jews from the empire. Haman persuaded King Ahasuerus that the Jews threatened the Persian empire's national security. As a result, he obtained a royal decree, setting aside a time for slaughtering the Jewish people. God had placed Esther in a situation in which she could make an astounding difference so long as she trusted Him. Mordecai challenged Esther with the truth that God had a specific purpose in placing her in her royal position. God will not fail to keep His promises or fall short of His purposes. Therefore, the deliverance of the Jews was certain. The only question was what Esther's role in that deliverance would be. God had made her queen so that she could deliver His people through her position and His provision. Esther's account serves as a reminder that God places people where they can serve Him.

H

E

A

R

T

Spend some time reflecting on what you have learned this week. Record a truth from each day that you want to remember, or go back and highlight portions of your journal.

DAY 1:

DAY 2:

DAY 3:

DAY 4:

DAY 5:

DAY 136 | ESTHER 5-7

MEMORY VERSES: DEUTERONOMY 29:29; PSALM 101:3-4

Esther eventually decided to intervene for her people. The stakes were high, and the risks were great. Even the queen could be put to death for coming into the king's presence without an invitation. As a result, Esther prepared herself through fasting and prayer. The Jewish people joined her by doing the same. After three days, Esther entered the king's court without being summoned. She invited the king and Haman to a banquet. Her patience gave time for God to work out the details of His plan for salvation. Time and again in Scripture we are reminded that God orchestrates even the most seemingly insignificant moments of our lives in order to bring Him glory. The many ironies in Esther 5-7 highlight this truth. Whereas Haman was expecting to be honored by his enemy Mordecai, it was Mordecai who would be publicly honored by Haman. Throughout it all, we are reminded of God's sovereign control over the details of our lives. As you reflect on the picture of God in these chapters of Scripture, remember that God is in control of your life, which means you can trust Him wholeheartedly.

H

E

A

R

T

WEEK AT A GLANCE
Today we pick back up in the story of Esther. As you read, look for evidence of how God used Esther to accomplish His purpose for His people. After we finish the book of Esther, we'll shift our attention to Nehemiah, who partnered with Ezra in the restoration of Jerusalem.

DAY 137 | ESTHER 8–10

MEMORY VERSES: DEUTERONOMY 29:29; PSALM 101:3-4

Esther exposed Haman's plot which led Ahasuerus to have him executed. The edict to kill the Jews remained in effect. Under Persian law Ahasuerus could not revoke it. Instead, the king issued a second edict authorizing Jews to arm and defend themselves, unleashing two days of violence as the two sides fought openly in its streets and fields. The Jews overcame their opposition, and afterward Mordecai ordered a celebration of these victories, which led to the establishment of the annual Festival of Purim. Because of the faithfulness of Esther and Mordecai, the Jewish people were protected, and God received the glory for everything He had done. Although the name of God is never explicitly mentioned in Esther, the book emphasizes the providence of God, the power of prayer and fasting, and the persuasive potential of courageous men and women of faith. God used Mordecai and Esther in a mighty way to preserve His covenant people—and with them, His ultimate plan of deliverance that would come nearly five centuries later in Jesus Christ. As their story reminds us, God receives glory when His people live in faithful obedience to Him.

H

E

A

R

T

MEMORY VERSES: DEUTERONOMY 29:29; PSALM 101:3-4

DAILY CHALLENGE

Like Ezra, Nehemiah was a man who answered God's call to leadership and played a key role in the restoration of Jerusalem and the people of Judah. Write down all the things you notice about Nehemiah's character and relationship with God from chapters 1–2. What does this teach you about being a person whom God can use?

The book of Nehemiah picks up where Ezra left off in the historical records of the restoration of Jerusalem. Under Ezra's spiritual leadership the Jews began to renew their allegiance to the Lord. Just thirteen years later Artaxerxes allowed another Jewish leader, Nehemiah, to return to the city. Nehemiah appeared with an ambitious goal: to rebuild the city's wall. Nearly a century had passed since the first Jewish exiles returned to Jerusalem. In that time they had constructed the temple and various other, mostly private structures. Yet even so, the defensive wall that surrounded the city remained to be rebuilt. The true problem wasn't a broken-down city. The true problem was a broken-down people who had a disconnected relationship with God. Nehemiah was called to rebuild a city and a community of people in shambles. Because of the exile, Jerusalem was in need of both physical and spiritual renewal. The same is true of our broken world. There are hurting and helpless people all around us—people who need the hope of Christ. When we let this reality sink in, like Nehemiah, we are compelled to step up and make a difference.

H

E

A

R

T

DAY 139 | NEHEMIAH 3-4

MEMORY VERSES: DEUTERONOMY 29:29; PSALM 101:3-4

The work to which God called Nehemiah would not be easy. And he could not do it alone. One reason the work progressed so quickly was that everyone took part. More intimidating than the physical obstacles was the human opposition. Not everyone was thrilled with Nehemiah's plan. In the Persian bureaucracy, lines of authority were not always clear, and some government officials feared that a stronger Jerusalem would diminish their prestige. For others, the development awakened ancient rivalries with the Jews. These enemies would seek to undermine Nehemiah with false accusations and duplicity. As a result, many people living in the vicinity were determined to spoil Nehemiah's plans. When we commit to faithfully serving God, He gives us big, God-sized goals to accomplish—goals that are only possible when we depend on Him. Often the bigger the goal, the bigger the opposition and challenges we face. No matter the source of our opposition, God gives us the strength to persevere and remain obedient to our tasks, as Nehemiah and the people of Jerusalem demonstrated for us.

H

E

A

R

T

THINK ABOUT IT

Opposition to God's plan is a thread you'll notice through all of Scripture, from Genesis 3 to Revelation 20. What is one area of your life in which you are seeking to be obedient to God yet are feeling opposition? How does Nehemiah's example speak to you?

MEMORY VERSE

Continue practicing the memory verse you chose. Write out as much of it as you can from memory, and then check to see how you did.

DAY 140 | NEHEMIAH 5–6

MEMORY VERSES: DEUTERONOMY 29:29; PSALM 101:3-4

WEEK IN REVIEW

Spend some time reflecting on what you have learned this week. Record a truth from each day that you want to remember, or go back and highlight portions of your journal.

DAY 1:

DAY 2:

DAY 3:

DAY 4:

DAY 5:

During the building program Nehemiah learned of social injustice among the Jewish population. The number of workers needed for rebuilding Jerusalem's wall was immense. The danger of attack required an equal number of men for military service. The economic strain created by the diversion of so many able-bodied workers from the regular labor force created an opportunity for corruption. Some Jews took advantage of other Jews to increase their profits. Nehemiah knew that the wall would not be completed unless the needs of the people were met. But more importantly, he knew that the rebuilding of the spiritual city would never be completed unless he faced the issues at hand. Despite external opposition and internal problems, the people continued to build the wall. Finally, the work was finished. It had taken only fifty-two days. From the beginning Nehemiah had put the matter of rebuilding Jerusalem's wall in God's hands. God's people had determined that the best answer to their opposition was to keep working and to fulfill God's will. As they did so, neighboring nations saw God's power at work in them. When God's people accomplish God's work in God's strength, God gets the glory.

H

E

A

R

T

DAY 141 | NEHEMIAH 7-8

MEMORY VERSES: NEHEMIAH 6:9; NEHEMIAH 9:6

Nehemiah 7-8 describes the first steps the people took after completion of the wall. The wall was necessary, but Jerusalem would not remain safe without people. In Nehemiah 8 we read that after people were settled, they devoted a day to hear the Word of God read to them from Ezra—a practice that was important because the people did not have prior access to Scripture. Even today, reading God's Word should be taken no less seriously. Through Scripture God reveals who He is and what a life lived in obedience to Him looks like. Scripture also provides countless stories of people who have gone before us in the faith and how God has proved faithful to His people time and time again. The most important thing we learn through Scripture, though, is the one big story it tells—the story of God's work to redeem His people and to draw them back to Him, which He accomplishes through the death, resurrection, and final victory of Jesus.

H

E

A

R

T

WEEK AT A GLANCE
This week we'll see what happened after the rebuilding of the wall around Jerusalem. Not only was it necessary to rebuild the wall, but the city also needed to be repopulated, and God had a plan for that too. Our reading wraps up at the end of this week with the celebration at the dedication of the wall.

DAY 142 | NEHEMIAH 9

MEMORY VERSES: NEHEMIAH 6:9; NEHEMIAH 9:6

DAILY CHALLENGE

After you've read and reflected on Nehemiah 9, look back over the prayer in verses 5-37 and note all of the action verbs associated with the Lord. Underline or circle them if you are able.

As the Israelites heard the Word of God read to them, they were reminded of God's faithfulness to His people and His plans, but they were also reminded of their unfaithfulness to Him. The sins of their ancestors were responsible for God's judgment against Jerusalem, which is what landed them in exile and necessitated the reconstruction of the city to begin with. Among the things Ezra's reading brought to light was the need for confession and repentance. Jesus once said, "Unless you repent, you will all perish as well" (Luke 13:3,5). Repentance can be defined as a heartfelt sorrow for sin, a renouncing of that sin, and a sincere commitment to turn from it and walk in obedience to Christ. Even as Christians, we often stumble away from the Lord by pursuing less than godly endeavors. We must accept responsibility for wandering away from God. No matter how badly we have stumbled in sin, the Lord lovingly invites us to return to Him. We cannot truly worship the Lord until we receive His forgiveness for the sin separating us from Him.

H

E

MEMORY VERSE

Pick one of the memory verse options for this week—Nehemiah 6:9; Nehemiah 9:6—and write the verse.

A

R

T

DAY 143 | NEHEMIAH 10

MEMORY VERSES: NEHEMIAH 6:9; NEHEMIAH 9:6

Nehemiah 9 involved a time of worship and confession, and it ended by mentioning a covenant the people made with God in light of His provisions and their repentance. The people's covenant with God expressed their commitment to living in obedience to Him and His laws. After renewing their commitment to obey God and His laws, chapter 10 includes several specific promises the people made to show how they would live out this commitment in daily life. The promises, which cover everything from Sabbath practices to sacrifice rituals to tithing, reinforce the idea that God has set apart the Israelites to be His chosen people, and as such, they are to live holy and set apart lives for Him. The goal is that they would be a witness to their community of the power and holiness of the one true God. Similarly, God calls us to live holy and set apart lives, which we do when we live in obedience to Him, pursue Christ, and allow the Holy Spirit to transform us. As God's chosen people today, we are to continue to live as a light for Him in our dark and broken world.

THINK ABOUT IT
Nehemiah 10 ends with the people stating: "We will not neglect the house of our God" (10:39). Ask the Lord to reveal specific ways you can more intentionally support your local church and its leaders.

H

E

A

R

T

DAY 144 | NEHEMIAH 11

MEMORY VERSES: NEHEMIAH 6:9; NEHEMIAH 9:6

THINK ABOUT IT

Think about where you live and where you work. What does your mission field look like? What needs are there? How might God have placed you uniquely there to fulfill those needs through Him?

After the work of rebuilding the wall was completed, God called certain people to relocate their families to Jerusalem and serve Him there. This was not necessarily the most desirable place to be. For most people, it meant relocating their families from the surrounding villages and uprooting their lives. Nehemiah instructed the people to cast lots to determine which families should go. Nehemiah 11 teaches that where you live and work matters to God. He has placed His people in specific places around specific people in order to serve Him uniquely. In his letter to the Colossian believers, Paul wrote, "Whatever you do, do it from the heart, as something done for the Lord and not for people" (Col. 3:23). This verse reminds us that for Christians, all of life is about glorifying God and serving Him—there should be no distinction between your secular duty and your sacred duty. Our attitude toward work makes a great deal of difference. As Christians, we can and should add an eternal dimension to our viewpoint. We know our ultimate reward for a job well done will come from the Lord.

MEMORY VERSE

Continue practicing the memory verse you chose. Write out as much of it as you can from memory, and then check to see how you did.

H

E

A

R

T

DAY 145 | NEHEMIAH 12

MEMORY VERSES: NEHEMIAH 6:9; NEHEMIAH 9:6

The completion of the wall and the repopulation of the city were celebrated with a dedication of the wall. This celebration included singing, ritual purification, and a procession around the wall that Nehemiah led. The people recognized that their ability to rebuild the wall so quickly amid such opposition was possible only because of the Lord, so they worshiped Him with songs of thanksgiving and praise. The climax of the celebration was the presentation of offerings to Him. We live in a culture that values individualism and a "pull yourself up by the bootstraps" mentality, which hinders us from acknowledging that even our best efforts and accomplishments are the result of God's blessing and provision in our lives. Every gift, talent, and opportunity you have is a result of God's desire to be glorified through your life, which He knows will alone lead to your greatest fulfillment and joy. Think about your offerings—everything from your monetary tithe to the way you spend your talents and time. Are you living as though God is the source of everything you have? If not, it's time to change that.

H

E

A

R

T

WEEK IN REVIEW

Spend some time reflecting on what you have learned this week. Record a truth from each day that you want to remember, or go back and highlight portions of your journal.

DAY 1:

DAY 2:

DAY 3:

DAY 4:

DAY 5:

DAY 146 | NEHEMIAH 13

MEMORY VERSES: PSALM 51:17; COLOSSIANS 1:19-20

The final chapter of Nehemiah concludes with an update from Nehemiah about what occurred in the newly revived city after he departed. Nehemiah was governor in Jerusalem for twelve years. On completing his mission, Nehemiah returned to Babylon to serve King Artaxerxes as he had promised. After serving the king for a season, Nehemiah's thoughts returned to Jerusalem. He was granted a second term as governor of the city, but when Nehemiah arrived back in the city, he discovered several violations of God's laws. The people strayed from the promises they made when they renewed their covenant with God. Once again Nehemiah found himself in the important position of spiritual leader, helping the people of God restore their relationship with Him. At its heart, the book of Nehemiah is about restoration—the restoration of a city and the restoration of the people of God. It begins and ends by challenging us to assess our spiritual lives, rid out the things that are separating us from pursuing God, and take the necessary steps toward restoration that come through trust and obedience.

H

E

A

R

T

WEEK AT A GLANCE
You may not have realized it yet, but this is your last week of reading in the Old Testament. You've made it to a big milestone in your year-long Bible reading journey! The New Testament and all the hope it brings is right around the corner. Let's finish this week strong!

DAY 147 | MALACHI 1

MEMORY VERSES: PSALM 51:17; COLOSSIANS 1:19-20

Malachi was the last of the Old Testament prophets. He prophesied at the same time Ezra and Nehemiah were leading God's people. Four centuries of prophetic silence followed his proclamation. The next prophet to speak in Scripture for the Lord would be John the Baptist. Malachi predicted John's coming and also the coming of Jesus Christ, the Messiah. God's last recorded word through His prophets before the coming of Jesus into the world was for His people to honor Him with their hearts and to serve Him faithfully with their lives. The book of Malachi begins with an emphasis on the greatness of God as seen in His love for His people in Israel. One of the first issues Malachi raised was God's accusation that Israel's priests disrespected Him by offering defiled sacrifices that were worthless. Those offerings revealed a contemptible attitude toward God. Malachi's warning reminds us that God's greatness requires from us a worthy gift and a loving giver. We need to have a wholehearted love for God and show that love through our actions and through worship that is worthy of His name.

H

E

A

R

T

THINK ABOUT IT

Malachi 1 closes with this statement from the Lord: "'For I am a great King,' says the LORD of Armies, 'and my name will be feared among the nations'" (v. 14). What does it mean to you to hear that God is a great King and the LORD of Armies? How should this part of His character affect your relationship with Him and the way you represent Him to those around you?

MEMORY VERSE

Pick one of the memory verse options for this week—Psalm 51:17; Colossians 1:19-20— and write the verse.

DAY 148 | MALACHI 2

MEMORY VERSES: PSALM 51:17; COLOSSIANS 1:19-20

THINK ABOUT IT

If those closest to you followed your example in worship, what would their worship look like?

What needs to change in the way you pursue God in worship?

In Malachi 2 the prophet addressed specific sins of the priests and the people who were both compromising their commitments to God, commitments that God takes very seriously. The priests were to revere God's name, give the people true instructions, live before God in peace and fairness, and turn the people from sin. They had done none of the above. Additionally, the people of Israel were the family of God; instead of honoring their family commitments to God and to one another, they were compromising those commitments by marrying people who worshiped idols and accepting their practices. God rebuked them and threatened to remove them from the community along with rejecting their worship. God has called us all to serve Him in some way. Whatever position or avenue of service you've accepted in response to God's leading is a covenant made with Him. God calls us to live honorably for Him by setting godly examples in our relationships and obligations, and Malachi's words remind us He takes it very seriously when we do not.

H

E

A

R

T

DAY 149 | MALACHI 3

MEMORY VERSES: PSALM 51:17; COLOSSIANS 1:19-20

At the close of Malachi 2, God charged His people with making Him weary by their words. The people charged God with injustice, an accusation that goes against His very character. He also accused them of robbing Him by not giving Him the tithes and offerings He is due. Sometimes we look at the state of the world around us and wonder if anything we do really makes a difference. We can understand where the people of Israel were coming from. They looked at the world around them and saw wicked people prospering, causing them to wonder what benefit there was to serving God. Like the Israelites, we often fail to recognize the goodness of God when things get difficult. It is into that discouraging place that God spoke a word of hope to His people—He would send His messenger (John the Baptist) and then He Himself would come to them and make things right, which He has done through Jesus. Today as we hold out hope for Jesus's promised return, God still expects His people to remain faithful to Him, which we demonstrate by serving God with right attitudes and right actions.

H

E

A

R

T

DAILY CHALLENGE
Malachi's name means "my messenger" or "Messenger of the Lord." As a disciple of Christ, you are God's messenger, too (Matt. 28:19-20). Set aside some time today to write out the message of God's love, the good news of the gospel, in your own words. Who needs to hear this good news from you today?

MEMORY VERSE
Continue practicing the memory verse you chose. Write out as much of it as you can from memory, and then check to see how you did.

WEEK IN REVIEW

You made it! Today is the last day of your Old Testament reading. I really hope you feel like you've learned more of the Old Testament and broadened your understanding of God's great story. Spend some time reflecting on what you have learned this week. Record a truth from each day that you want to remember, or go back and highlight portions of your journal.

DAY 1:

DAY 2:

DAY 3:

DAY 4:

DAY 5:

DAY 150 | MALACHI 4

MEMORY VERSES: PSALM 51:17; COLOSSIANS 1:19-20

At the close of Malachi's prophecy, God reminded the people that a final day of judgment and blessing was coming. God described this as a day when the wicked (those who did not follow God) would be consumed and the righteous (those who follow God) would be healed and their victory over evil complete. Before that day Elijah would appear to prepare people for the coming day. About five centuries after Malachi lived, both an angel (Luke 1:16-17) and Jesus (Matt. 17:10-13) confirmed that John the Baptist fulfilled Malachi's prophecy of an Elijah who was to come. John was not Elijah in such a literal sense (John 1:21). Instead, John the Baptist was zealous for the Lord as Elijah was, turned people back to the Lord as Elijah did, and prepared the way for the Lord to come to His people as Elijah exemplified. Tucked into these final verses of the Old Testament is the hope of the gospel. The only thing that could finally preserve people from God's judgment against sin is for Jesus to bear the curse for us. He accomplished this in His death on the cross in fulfillment of Malachi's prophecy.

H

E

A

R

T

DAY 151 | LUKE 1

MEMORY VERSES: JOHN 1:1-2; JOHN 1:14

For centuries God spoke through His prophets. Then after Malachi He stopped talking. For nearly five hundred years God remained silent. All of the promises God made seemed to be fading away in the hearts of His people. God did not remain silent forever. He spoke again through John the Baptist, a prophet who had the unique responsibility of announcing that Jesus, the long-awaited Messiah, had arrived. Luke began his Gospel (his account of the events surrounding Jesus's earthly ministry) with the angelic announcements of two key births—John the Baptist's and Jesus's. The birth stories of these two people were intricately linked. The angel's descriptions of both men reveal key information about who Jesus is and why He came. Jesus is the very Son of God, and His name means "Deliverer" or "Savior." He came to save God's people from their bondage to sin and to establish the kingdom of God—His justice and righteousness—on earth. The announcement of Jesus's birth shows that, despite present conditions, God had not and would never abandon His people—a truth we need constant reminders of today.

H

E

A

R

T

WEEK AT A GLANCE
As we begin our time in the New Testament, it's important to remember that more than four hundred years of silence from God went by between the prophets Malachi and John the Baptist. John comes on the scene proclaiming the good news of Jesus Christ, the Messiah who the entire Old Testament points toward. I hope you're excited about what's to come.

DAY 152 | LUKE 2

MEMORY VERSES: JOHN 1:1-2; JOHN 1:14

THINK ABOUT IT

One of my favorite verses is Luke 2:52. It shows us that Jesus grew in four distinct ways: "And Jesus increased in wisdom [intellectually] and stature [physically], and in favor with God [spiritually] and with people [socially]." If Jesus grew in these ways while on earth, shouldn't we desire to as well and teach others to do the same?

Luke 2 provides the account of Jesus's birth and childhood. Mary gave birth to Jesus in Bethlehem, an event that became a reason for celebration by the greatest and the least in heaven and on earth. An angel reported the good news to shepherds with a heavenly host singing God's praises. After Jesus's birth, Mary and Joseph fulfilled the important Jewish rites of the circumcision and purification sacrifice at the temple in Jerusalem. At age twelve, Jesus traveled with Mary and Joseph to the temple. He spent time dialoguing with the teachers, who were amazed at His wisdom. He then returned with His family to Nazareth. From the very beginning of Jesus's story, we learn that God's Son would not fit people's expectations of the Messiah, the great Deliverer and Conqueror of the Jews. In fact, we quickly realize that the invitation to know Jesus extends to everyone, regardless of class, education, race, or position. God has limitless, unconditional, and equal love for all of us. Likewise, we're called to have the same unconditional mindset as we're sent out to share the gospel.

H

E

A

MEMORY VERSE

Pick one of the memory verse options for this week—John 1:1-2; John 1:14—and write the verse.

R

T

Each of the Gospels gives a detailed account of Jesus's time on earth; however, each Gospel writer had a unique purpose for writing, and that purpose shaped which encounters and teachings they included. It also determined how they began and ended their Gospels. The Gospel of Matthew is written to a Jewish audience who had an understanding of the Old Testament Scriptures. This explains why Matthew began with Jesus's genealogy. The genealogy affirms that Jesus descended from Abraham, Judah, and David, fulfilling various Old Testament prophecies about the Messiah. Following the genealogy, Matthew focuses on events surrounding Jesus's birth. The angel's appearance to Joseph in a dream with the message of the miraculous conception underscores Jesus's divine nature. The wise men's search, discovery, and subsequent worship of Jesus further confirms His identity. Even the family's escape to Egypt, eventual return to Israel, and their settling in the city of Nazareth is again a prophetic fulfillment. From reading the birth and infancy narratives in Matthew, we are reminded that God keeps His promises. We also learn that Jesus was God's unique Son and that He alone is positioned to change the world.

THINK ABOUT IT

Reread Jesus's genealogy in Matthew 1:1-17. Count the number of women included in it. Each of these women—Tamar, Rahab, Ruth, Bathsheba, and Mary—lived complicated lives, yet their stories are told in Scripture and they forever hold a significant place in the lineage of the Messiah. Jesus truly came to save everyone, and no one is outside of the reach of His love. Offer a prayer of gratitude and praise to the Lord for Jesus's love for you.

H

E

A

R

T

DAY 154 | MARK 1

MEMORY VERSES: JOHN 1:1-2; JOHN 1:14

DAILY CHALLENGE

After you complete today's journal entry, look back over your notes from Days 151–153. On a separate piece of paper, make a chart listing the similarities and differences between the openings to each of the Synoptic Gospels (Matthew, Mark, and Luke).

Unlike the other three Gospels, Mark begins abruptly at the start of Jesus's earthly ministry, thirty years after His birth. Much of Mark's Gospel focuses on the actions of Jesus and how people responded to Him. The chapter begins with information about the preparations made for Jesus's ministry. John the Baptist called for repentance from sin and proclaimed the One (Jesus) to follow. Jesus presented Himself for baptism to John as a way of affirming John's ministry. Mark next introduced Jesus as proclaimer of the message of good news with a call to repentance. Jesus issues a formal invitation to four fishermen to follow Him. Jesus further demonstrated His oneness with God as He displayed authority over unclean spirits and healed many physical illnesses. Although many people sought Him because of His healing power, Jesus shied away from the crowds and devoted most of His time to training the twelve disciples. A final healing, however, shows Jesus's ministry to be marked by compassion toward those in need. From the beginning of Mark's Gospel, we see that in Jesus's ministry, meeting people's spiritual and physical needs go hand in hand. This is the model He demonstrates for us.

H

E

MEMORY VERSE

Continue practicing the memory verse you chose. Write out as much of it as you can from memory, and then check to see how you did.

A

R

T

DAY 155 | JOHN 1

MEMORY VERSES: JOHN 1:1-2; JOHN 1:14

John 1 focuses on Jesus's divinity and role in creation as well as the start of His earthly ministry. The Word, Jesus, is divine, distinct from God the Father but one with Him. God created everything through the Word. Nothing came into being without His direct involvement. Life came through Jesus, who provided the light of God's love and guidance. As the creation of physical light dispelled the darkness on the first day of creation (Gen. 1:3), so Jesus's light pierced through the darkness of sin to provide eternal salvation to those who believe in Him. Although the world had been created through the Word, the world's people did not recognize or respond to Him. Despite that rejection, some accepted Jesus, believing in Him as Savior. In addition, John's Gospel also emphasizes the humanity of Jesus. By coming in human form, Jesus allowed us to see the glory of God. John the Baptist's witness proved true as the life, ministry, death, and resurrection of Jesus revealed God's grace and truth. In Him we find grace, truth, and salvation. Like the first disciples who answered Jesus's call to follow Him, once Christ changes our lives, we are compelled to demonstrate the power of the gospel, pointing others to Jesus.

H

E

A

R

T

WEEK IN REVIEW

As we spend this next half of the year learning about Jesus, let's pray now for God to reveal Himself to us. Remember, we want to live by the Bible, not just know information about the Bible. Spend some time reflecting on what you have learned this week. Record a truth from each day that you want to remember, or go back and highlight portions of your journal.

DAY 1:

DAY 2:

DAY 3:

DAY 4:

DAY 5:

DAY 156 | MATTHEW 3-4

MEMORY VERSES: MATTHEW 5:16; MATTHEW 6:33

Before Jesus begins His public ministry, Matthew introduces John the Baptist, who prepared the way for Jesus by proclaiming a message of repentance and calling people to baptism as a symbol of their heart transformation. Jesus travels to the river for John to baptize Him. By being baptized, Jesus identified Himself with John's message and with the people He came to save. It is interesting to note that all three Persons of the Trinity show up for this important moment in Jesus's ministry, which affirms that Jesus is the Son of God and that His mission is anointed by the Holy Spirit. After His baptism, Jesus endured a time of temptation in the desert. This preparation for ministry reveals the reality of the spiritual battle raging around us and provides for us a concrete example of how God equips us to withstand temptations. When we face temptations, we too can trust in the character of God and the promises of Scripture, no matter how appealing that temptation might be.

H

E

A

R

T

WEEK AT A GLANCE
The launch of Jesus's public ministry takes center stage in our readings in Matthew's Gospel this week. Included in the text we'll read is the Sermon on the Mount, a life-changing sermon preached by Jesus Himself. Enjoy, friends!

DAY 157 | MATTHEW 5

MEMORY VERSES: MATTHEW 5:16; MATTHEW 6:33

After Jesus's time in the desert, He launched into His public ministry by proclaiming the message that the kingdom of God was at hand, choosing His disciples, and preaching to and healing the crowds. In Matthew 5 the Gospel shifts to the record of Jesus's Sermon on the Mount—His teaching on how citizens of the kingdom of God should conduct themselves. The sermon begins with the Beatitudes, blessings from God that emphasize the inner motives rather than mere outward conformity. Jesus then shifted His message to the issue of behavior. Jesus addressed several Jewish laws and helped His disciples understand how right behavior is never the ultimate indicator. A person must have the right heart motive too. The commands of God remind us that He has a plan for how we ought to live our lives, and that plan is based in who He is and how He has treated us. Ultimately, we must remember that the God who demands perfection has already provided a means through the perfect sacrifice of His Son, Jesus.

H

E

A

R

T

MEMORY VERSE

Pick one of the memory verse options for this week—Matthew 5:16; Matthew 6:33—and write the verse.

DAILY CHALLENGE

Prayer is the primary way we communicate with God. Take the truths you wrote down in your journaling time and incorporate them into your prayers this week.

DAY 158 | MATTHEW 6

MEMORY VERSES: MATTHEW 5:16; MATTHEW 6:33

As Jesus continued His Sermon on the Mount, He taught that religious behaviors—specifically giving, praying, and fasting—can be carried out through healthy or unhealthy motives. The inappropriate motive focuses on recognition and attention, while the appropriate motive is aimed at sacrifice and worship of God. Included in this teaching is Jesus's well-known Model Prayer, which highlights prayer as a means of worshiping God, aligning ourselves with His will, and depending on Him to meet our daily physical and spiritual needs. The rest of Matthew 6 addresses our priorities from a kingdom perspective. Jesus was particularly concerned with showing how anxiety and worry can prevent us from receiving the full benefit of God's blessing. This is important because our priorities get the bulk of our time and attention, and they reveal our level of trust in God. Kingdom people should aspire to a singular focus on God and a loyalty to Him. Worry is the opposite of trust in God.

H

E

A

R

T

DAY 159 | MATTHEW 7

MEMORY VERSES: MATTHEW 5:16; MATTHEW 6:33

Relationships are the focus of the next section of the Sermon on the Mount. Jesus teaches that His kingdom people are not to be judgmental and condemning of others. The loving relationship we enjoy with God sets the standard for our relationships with others. Jesus also taught that prayer is the primary way we function in relationship with God, and He wants us to continually approach Him with our requests. He delights to give us what we need. Jesus specifically teaches that our prayers are powerful when we are persistent, when we believe God's promises, and when we trust God's heart. Jesus's sermon builds to a climactic ending in chapter 7, when He challenged His listeners to make a choice—would they follow Him through the narrow gate into the kingdom, or would they choose the wide gate that many enter which leads to ultimate destruction? The true Christian is marked by obedience that flows from a real, personal relationship with Jesus Christ.

H

E

A

R

T

THINK ABOUT IT
Consider the following questions after reading Matthew 7. How would your relationship with God and others be different if you lived the way Jesus sets forth in this passage?

What is one obstacle you currently face in doing so?

MEMORY VERSE
Continue practicing the memory verse you chose. Write out as much of it as you can from memory, and then check to see how you did.

DAY 160 | MATTHEW 8

MEMORY VERSES: MATTHEW 5:16; MATTHEW 6:33

WEEK IN REVIEW

Spend some time reflecting on what you have learned this week. Record a truth from each day that you want to remember, or go back and highlight portions of your journal.

DAY 1:

DAY 2:

DAY 3:

DAY 4:

DAY 5:

After the Sermon on the Mount, Matthew's Gospel returns to Jesus's ministry, which was marked by miraculous healings and wonders. Matthew 8 records three miracles of healing that demonstrated slightly different aspects of Jesus's power. The cleansing of the leper demonstrated Jesus's power over one of the worst maladies of the day. The healing of the centurion's servant showed that Jesus did not need to be physically present to heal. At Capernaum Jesus cast out demons, which demonstrated His sovereign power over evil. After those healings, Jesus illustrated the true nature of discipleship. True discipleship is defined by trust in Jesus, no matter what the circumstances may be. The next two miracles, the calming of the storm and the two men possessed by multiple demons, demonstrate Jesus's power over nature itself and over the most extensive and entrenched evil. The complete picture of Jesus's power on display in Matthew 8 shows that through Christ the God of the universe transforms individual lives.

H

E

A

R

T

DAY 161 | LUKE 9:10-62

MEMORY VERSES: LUKE 14:26-27; LUKE 14:33

Luke 9 is one of the most important chapters of Scripture related to understanding what it means to be a disciple of Jesus. This chapter includes a combination of teachings and miracles from Jesus that provide instruction and demonstration of His ministry in action. Jesus showed His concern for people's physical needs when He fed the hungry crowd. Later He also displayed His power over evil and the supernatural realm by healing a boy sickened by demon possession. Through Jesus's conversations with His disciples in this chapter, we learn about His true identity and mission as the Son of God, the Messiah, who would die and be resurrected as the atonement for sin. Jesus's transfiguration with Moses and Elijah validated God's approval of His Son and the mission He was living out. As Jesus's disciples, we are challenged to live a life of self-denial focused on selfless service of others. Jesus did not sugarcoat discipleship; instead, He taught that following Him is about putting the needs of others—both physical and spiritual—ahead of our own.

H

E

A

R

T

WEEK AT A GLANCE
We'll be reading from multiple Gospels this week for a well-rounded look into what took place in Jesus's earthly ministry. The events and conversations that will unfold—including Jesus's transfiguration and a nighttime chat with Nicodemus—teach us invaluable spiritual truths.

DAY 162 | MARK 9–10

The dictionary defines *faith* as "complete trust or confidence in someone or something."[13] God's definition of faith is "the reality of what is hoped for, the proof of what is not seen" (Heb. 11:1). Come up with your own definition of *faith* in God, and write it below.

MEMORY VERSE

Pick one of the memory verse options for this week—Luke 14:26-27; Luke 14:33—and write the verse.

After Jesus's prediction of His suffering, death, and resurrection and His rebuke of Peter, Jesus spoke about the duty of those who follow Him. Before the glory of salvation comes suffering. Because of the great level of sacrifice required, it is important that we understand who Jesus is, which was the very point of His transfiguration. On a high mountain Jesus was transformed in the midst of Peter, James, and John. Elijah and Moses joined Him. Jesus used this event to inform the disciples further about His coming death and victorious resurrection. As soon as they came down from the mountain, these men were reminded of the importance of faith in God as the foundation for ministry. A desperate father asked the disciples to cast a demon out of his deaf and mute son. They tried and failed. When Jesus discovered their inability to cast out the demon, He attributed it to a lack of faith on their part. By contrast, the father displayed faith as he trusted Jesus to heal the boy. No matter what Jesus calls you to do and what sacrifice is required as His disciple, the most important thing is that you put your faith and trust in Him as you live out that call.

H

E

A

R

T

DAY 163 | LUKE 12

MEMORY VERSES: LUKE 14:26-27; LUKE 14:33

Throughout Jesus's earthly ministry He taught His followers truths to live by. Among the practical teachings in Luke 12, Jesus encouraged His followers to avoid hypocrisy by revering God and by boldly confessing Jesus before others. He also told a parable to warn them about greed and worry. The life of a child of God should be one marked by trust in Him as the ultimate Provider and Protector. Throughout Scripture God proves time and again that He takes care of His children. He also reminds us that this world is not our home, so the temporary things wrapped up in it should not lead to fear or worry. The temporary nature of this world is the point of Jesus's parable on expectantly awaiting the Master's return. For disciples of Jesus, this world is about anticipating and preparing for eternity. Our emphasis in the meantime should be on a life of obedience to Christ and participation in His gospel ministry.

DAILY CHALLENGE
Write a prayer of gratitude to God for being your Provider:

Now write a prayer of gratitude to God for being your Protector:

H

E

A

R

T

DAY 164 | JOHN 3-4

MEMORY VERSES: LUKE 14:26-27; LUKE 14:33

DAILY CHALLENGE

An encounter with Jesus changes a person for eternity. In a separate journal or on another piece of paper, write out your testimony—your story of coming to know Jesus—and reflect on how God has changed you through your relationship with Him.

MEMORY VERSE

Continue practicing the memory verse you chose. Write out as much of it as you can from memory, and then check to see how you did.

John 3–4 includes two important conversations Jesus had with two very different individuals—a Pharisee named Nicodemus and a Samaritan woman. Jesus's conversation with Nicodemus (John 3) sheds light on what is required for a person to become a part of the kingdom of God, which takes place through a relationship with Jesus. At the heart of Jesus's teaching is the concept of being born again, which speaks to the life-changing effect of the Holy Spirit in a person's life. This change takes place as a person confesses belief that Jesus is the Son of God, who died to pay the price for his or her sins. That confession makes way for the forgiving power of God's grace. In John 4 Jesus described the new life available in Him as living water in His conversation with the woman at the well. The image of living water that forever satisfies a person's thirst speaks to eternal life with God—one of the benefits of salvation from sin through Jesus. Both of these spiritual conversations give us insight into salvation and the benefits it brings, and both remind us that Jesus is central to salvation. Only a relationship with Him brings the spiritual satisfaction and fulfillment we desire.

H

E

A

R

T

DAY 165 | LUKE 14

MEMORY VERSES: LUKE 14:26-27; LUKE 14:33

In Luke 14 Jesus told two parables in a banquet setting to teach the need for humility. Through these parables we learn that God values and honors a humble spirit that seeks to put others ahead of oneself. This is the very example Jesus modeled for us. He left His position with God the Father in heaven and came to earth in order to make a way for sinful humanity to be reunited with God. His actions required humility on many levels, culminating at the cross, where the very Son of God died for us. Jesus is our model for a life of humble service in the kingdom of God. A third parable about a king going to battle anticipated disciples counting the cost before following Jesus. In order to be obedient to Jesus's call to discipleship, we must prioritize Him and His mission above everything else in life—even above life itself.

H

E

A

R

T

Spend some time reflecting on what you have learned this week. Record a truth from each day that you want to remember, or go back and highlight portions of your journal.

DAY 1:

DAY 2:

DAY 3:

DAY 4:

DAY 5:

DAY 166 | JOHN 6

MEMORY VERSES: MARK 10:45; JOHN 6:37

While there are many points of similarity between the four Gospels, there are also considerable differences because each Gospel writer had a unique message he wanted to communicate to a particular audience. Among the teachings and content unique to John's Gospel are the "I am" statements of Jesus, the first of which appears in John 6. With each of these statements, Jesus reveals His attributes. In John 6 Jesus said, "I am the bread of life" (v. 35). He declared this immediately after miraculously feeding a large crowd. By meeting the people's physical need for food and then declaring Himself to be the Bread of Life, Jesus helps us see that He alone can satisfy our spiritual hunger. Everyone is born with spiritual hunger, whether or not they recognize it, and people attempt to supplement many things to fill this spiritual void, including religion, materialism, and relationships. But the only thing capable of satisfying a person's spiritual hunger is to know Jesus as his or her loving Savior.

H

E

A

WEEK AT A GLANCE
This week we'll continue reading from each of the Gospels. We'll read about parables, possessions, and prayer. Ask the Lord to speak directly to your heart as you begin.

R

T

DAY 167 | MATTHEW 19:16-30

MEMORY VERSES: MARK 10:45; JOHN 6:37

Matthew 19:16-30 tells about Jesus's conversation with a man known only as the rich young ruler. This man approached Jesus during a time when He was teaching and inquired about the necessary requirements for eternal life with God. In response, Jesus told the man to sell all of his possessions and give the money to the poor. Although the man was faithful to obey the law, he refused to give up everything to follow Jesus, which left him outside of the kingdom of God. Jesus's instruction to this man highlighted the idols in his life—his money and possessions mattered greatly to him. They were his whole identity. However, Jesus teaches time and again that nothing can have a greater priority in our lives than following Jesus, and our faith in God should be the source of our identity. Through His conversation with the rich young ruler, Jesus revealed that He knows our hearts, and He also knows what we are tempted to place above Him.

DAILY CHALLENGE
Now that you've read about Jesus's encounter with the rich young ruler, think through these questions:

What do you sense God telling you to sacrifice in order to be a more committed disciple?

H

E

What is the first step you need to take to be obedient to Him?

A

MEMORY VERSE
Pick one of the memory verse options for this week—Mark 10:45; John 6:37—and write the verse.

R

T

DAY 168 | LUKE 15–16

MEMORY VERSES: MARK 10:45; JOHN 6:37

KEY WORD: PARABLE

Jesus told more than forty-five parables, and some are included in each of the Gospels. Luke includes more parables in his book than the other writers. This type of teaching was a great tool for Jesus, because it allowed Him to use everyday imagery—things people could see/touch/feel—to teach spiritual truths—things people couldn't see.

In Luke 15–16 Jesus used a series of parables (an illustrative story used to communicate spiritual truth) to teach His listeners important lessons about His relationship with us and how we are to live in response to Him. The three parables in Luke 15, often referred to as the lost parables, describe the joy associated with the repentance of sinners. All of heaven rejoices when people turn to God through faith in Jesus. These parables remind us that all people matter to God and that their salvation should matter to us too. As the parable of the prodigal son demonstrates, no sin is so great that it can keep us out of reach of God's loving grace. Once we experience salvation, everything changes, including how we live day to day and how we view the things of this world. That new perspective is central to the parables and teachings in Luke 16, which have to do with handling money. In the kingdom of God, money can serve a good purpose when used properly. When viewed from the wrong perspective, however, money can blind a person from that which matters most—a right relationship with God.

H

E

A

R

T

DAY 169 | LUKE 17:11-37; 18

MEMORY VERSES: MARK 10:45; JOHN 6:37

One of the themes that surfaces time and again in the Gospels is that salvation changes us. A story in Luke 10 tells about ten lepers who were healed by Jesus. Of the ten, only one returned to thank Him, but that one revealed the truth that understanding the change Jesus has brought about in our lives should lead to a heart of gratitude toward Him. Prayer also played a significant role in Jesus's life and teaching. At the start of Luke 18, we read a story Jesus told about a widow, which highlights the need for persistence in prayer, even when it seems like God is being slow to answer us (2 Pet. 3:9). A second parable about the Pharisee and the tax collector emphasizes the need for humility in prayer. Both persistence and humility in prayer communicate total dependency on God and a desire to unite with Him through prayer. Prayer is one of the greatest gifts God gives His children and is a gift for which we, like the leper, should be eternally grateful.

H

E

A

R

T

THINK ABOUT IT

"The Lord does not delay his promise, as some understand delay, but is patient with you, not wanting any to perish but all to come to repentance."

–2 Peter 3:9

MEMORY VERSE

Continue practicing the memory verse you chose. Write out as much of it as you can from memory, and then check to see how you did.

DAY 170 | MARK 10

MEMORY VERSES: MARK 10:45; JOHN 6:37

WEEK IN REVIEW

Spend some time reflecting on what you have learned this week. Record a truth from each day that you want to remember, or go back and highlight portions of your journal.

DAY 1:

DAY 2:

DAY 3:

DAY 4:

DAY 5:

Many times during His earthly ministry, Jesus predicted His own death and the suffering His disciples would endure. He wanted those who followed Him to have a clear picture of what they were getting themselves into—connecting oneself with the mission of Jesus requires sacrifice. Contrary to how the disciples viewed it, Jesus defined effective discipleship by the practice of humble service to other people (Mark 10:42-45). He downplayed success as an attainment of position and power. Real effectiveness in ministry comes through serving, not through being served. This mindset was countercultural in Jesus's day, and it remains countercultural for ours today too. Serving others requires an active attentiveness to people's needs and genuine compassion for people's souls. When we struggle to show this kind of humility and compassion to others, it is important to remember that this is how God loves us. Recognizing the love, compassion, and grace of God in our own lives enables us to overflow that love to others.

H

E

A

R

T

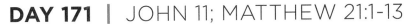

DAY 171 | JOHN 11; MATTHEW 21:1-13

MEMORY VERSES: JOHN 13:34-35; JOHN 15:4-5

John 11 records one of Jesus's greatest miracles—raising Lazarus from the dead. Lazarus, the brother of Mary and Martha, featured prominently in Jesus's life and ministry, died and was buried before Jesus arrived to heal him. However, Lazarus's death gave Jesus the opportunity to further establish His authority by showing that He even has authority over death, something only God Himself can claim. Another "I am" statement in John's Gospel is found in this account: Jesus said, "I am the resurrection and the life" (John 11:25). This means that only through a relationship with Jesus is eternal life in God's presence possible. After this miracle the threat against Jesus's life intensified and the cross drew nearer. Matthew 21:1-13 describes Jesus's triumphal entry into Jerusalem and the cleansing of the temple, which highlighted further His authority and identity as the Messiah, the promised Son of God. The triumphal entry also marked the beginning of the end of Jesus's earthly ministry, as His death on the cross loomed near.

H

E

A

R

T

WEEK AT A GLANCE
This week starts off with a bang! We'll read about Jesus's dear friend Lazarus rising from the dead. There is so much to learn in this passage alone, and this is only Day 1 of the week. We'll also read about Jesus washing the disciples' feet and their time together in the upper room.

DAY 172 | JOHN 13

THINK ABOUT IT

One mark of a disciple of Jesus is love for others. Survey the way you've loved others lately, from your family to your friends, to coworkers and strangers. What does your degree of love for others communicate about God's love and your relationship to Him?

Jesus's sacrificial death occupies a central focus in John's Gospel, as everything moves toward a climax at the cross and a triumph through the resurrection. The first twelve chapters of John's Gospel focus on Jesus's life, teachings, and ministry. With chapter 13 the focus shifts to His final meal with His disciples before His arrest, death, resurrection, and appearances to believers. At this moment in Jesus's ministry, He turned His attention to His disciples, both to prepare them for the coming events and to teach them the kingdom qualities of humility, service, and love. In spite of His knowledge about Judas's betrayal, Peter's denial, and the general unfaithfulness of the disciples, Jesus demonstrated a servant's attitude toward His disciples on the evening prior to His arrest. He washed His disciples' feet and utilized that experience as a time to teach His disciples about loving and humble service. Today, Jesus continues to call His followers to imitate His example, even when serving is uncomfortable and inconvenient.

H

E

MEMORY VERSE

Pick one of the memory verse options for this week—John 13:34-35; John 15:4-5—and write the verse.

A

R

T

DAY 173 | JOHN 14–15

MEMORY VERSES: JOHN 13:34-35; JOHN 15:4-5

After Jesus washed the disciples' feet, He continued to outline expectations for each of them after His death. Anticipating the sorrow His disciples would experience at His departure, Jesus offered a message of comfort and consolation to enable them to live confidently. In another of Jesus's "I am" statements, He referred to Himself as "the way, the truth, and the life" (John 14:6). Jesus is the single reliable source of redemptive revelation. Apart from Him, there is no means of knowing God and no hope of abundant, eternal life. One more "I am" statement is found in John 15, when Jesus said, "I am the true vine" (v. 1). The imagery in this chapter describes Jesus's relationship with believers in two ways: (1) vine and branches and (2) master and friends. As branches, we have the responsibility of abiding in Him so we can experience a productive life. As friends, we have the privilege of understanding His mission for us and through us as we obey His commands.

THINK ABOUT IT

"You are the branch. You need be nothing more. You need not for one single moment of the day take upon you the responsibility of the Vine. You need not leave the place of entire dependence and unbounded confidence."[14]

—Andrew Murray, from *The True Vine*

H

E

A

R

T

DAY 174 | JOHN 16

MEMORY VERSES: JOHN 13:34-35; JOHN 15:4-5

DAILY CHALLENGE

One of the key takeaways from John 16 is this: Sorrow and suffering are temporary, but the joy of the Lord will last forever. What are some of the many troubles you are currently facing? How might Jesus's statement that He has overcome the world enable you to "be courageous" as He commands?

MEMORY VERSE

Continue practicing the memory verse you chose. Write out as much of it as you can from memory, and then check to see how you did.

In the final instructions given to His disciples in the upper room on the night before His crucifixion (John 13–16), Jesus promised that He would ask the Father to send the Holy Spirit to His disciples (14:15-17). He revealed that the Holy Spirit would be their Counselor (14:25-26). The Holy Spirit would testify about Jesus Christ and enable believers to testify also (15:26-27). The Spirit's ministry to the world would be to convict people of sin, righteousness, and judgment in His efforts to bring them to faith and salvation in Jesus Christ (16:5-15). The Holy Spirit would guide believers into all truth. Genuine spirituality involves growing in a personal knowledge of and experience with the person and ministry of the Holy Spirit in our daily lives. Only through the Spirit's strength are we able to find the hope and confidence Jesus encourages at the close of this chapter with the words "Be courageous! I have conquered the world" (John 16:33).

H

E

A

R

T

DAY 175 | MATTHEW 24:1-31

MEMORY VERSES: JOHN 13:34-35; JOHN 15:4-5

Matthew 24 contains several teachings from Jesus concerning the future. As His death drew closer, Jesus knew the disciples needed to be prepared for the suffering and persecution that would eventually come, and He also knew they needed a reason to maintain hope when things grew challenging. Jesus prophesied about the fall of the temple, which took place in AD 70. To the disciples' question concerning signs of the end, Jesus replied that we should not misinterpret the signs. Persecutions of various types are to be expected. False messiahs will arise. People will be deceived. All of these things are preludes to the end of the age, when Jesus Himself will return and right the world once and for all. It can be hard to process teachings like these from Jesus because the final days come with so much uncertainty, but the most important takeaway is that Jesus will return again. We must be ready when He does.

H

E

A

R

T

WEEK IN REVIEW
Spend some time reflecting on what you have learned this week. Record a truth from each day that you want to remember, or go back and highlight portions of your journal.

DAY 1:

DAY 2:

DAY 3:

DAY 4:

DAY 5:

DAY 176 | MATTHEW 24:32-51

MEMORY VERSES: LUKE 23:34; JOHN 17:3

One of the things Scripture teaches us time and again is that the end times will be a time of judgment. This is good news for people who know Jesus as their Savior and Lord, but it is bad news for people who do not have a personal relationship with Him. In Matthew 24 Jesus illustrated the certainty of judgment with the parable of the fig tree and warned against trying to predict the time of His return. The real need is not for insight to read the times, but perseverance to remain faithful and dedication to the mission of drawing more people to Christ. While we wait for Jesus to return, we must be about the work of spreading the gospel so that as many people as possible can have the hope and promise of eternal life with Jesus.

H

E

A

R

T

WEEK AT A GLANCE

This week we read one of my favorite passages of Scripture, John 17. This passage is known as the high priestly prayer in which Jesus prayed for His disciples the night of His arrest. We'll also reach the moment all of Scripture has been building toward—Jesus's crucifixion and burial.

DAY 177 | JOHN 17

John 17 is referred to as Jesus's high priestly prayer. Jesus's prayer on the eve of His arrest and trials includes a prayer for Himself, a prayer for His disciples, and a prayer for future believers of every age. Jesus's prayer for Himself was that He would glorify His Father through His death. He then prayed that His disciples would glorify the Father by preserving the unity they had in Jesus. Within this section of the prayer, Jesus petitioned the Father to protect His disciples from the evil one. Finally, Jesus prayed for all who would come to believe in Him in the future. He wanted these believers to experience unity and grow in knowledge and love. By demonstrating unity, unbelievers would respond to the proclamation of the gospel while believers glorify the Father. Jesus's selfless prayer is a model for all of us.

DAILY CHALLENGE

Take some time to write your own prayer, using Jesus's prayer in John 17 as a guide. Grab another piece of paper if you want more room to write.

H

E

A

R

T

MEMORY VERSE

Pick one of the memory verse options for this week—Luke 23:34; John 17:3—and write the verse.

DAY 178 | MATTHEW 26:35–27:31

MEMORY VERSES: LUKE 23:34; JOHN 17:3

READ ON

Jesus, our Savior, is the thread who runs throughout all of Scripture. Matthew points readers back to the following Old Testament prophecies coming true in Jesus:

• Psalm 110:1
• Jeremiah 32:6-9
• Daniel 7:13
• Zechariah 11:12-13

After Jesus finished the Passover meal and wrapped up His teachings, the events of the crucifixion night were set in motion. While Jesus retreated to pray, Judas—one of Jesus's own disciples—showed up with an army of people to arrest Him. Jesus was immediately escorted to trial before the high priest. Chapter 26 ends with Jesus being condemned by the Sanhedrin and Peter denying that he even knew Him. Matthew 27 concentrates on Jesus's trial and death. Through injustice and persecution, Jesus remained humble and steadfast in His obedience to the will of the Father. Jesus's interrogation ended with Pilate granting the religious leaders' request to sentence Jesus to crucifixion in place of Barabbas, a guilty criminal. With that verdict, Jesus, in His innocence, was delivered over to death, just as was prophesied. We are all like Barabbas—sinful people who stand guilty before God but for whom Jesus gave His life in order to pay the price that our sinfulness demands. Because He died, we can live.

H

E

A

R

T

DAY 179 | MATTHEW 27:32-66; LUKE 23:26-56

MEMORY VERSES: LUKE 23:34; JOHN 17:3

Today's readings from Matthew and Luke give the account of Jesus's death on the cross, the event up to which His entire ministry had been leading. Crucifixion was the most painful and barbaric form of capital punishment in ancient times. The Romans at first used it only for slaves; later for enemies of the state; and by the first century, as a deterrent for criminal activity. Jesus was none of these. However, His sacrificial death was always God's plan. Jesus's crucifixion produced different responses from those who saw it. One of the two criminals crucified alongside Jesus insulted Him, while the other asked for His forgiveness. The religious leaders and soldiers mocked Him. A centurion confessed Jesus's righteous nature. Among the Gospel writers, only Luke reported Jesus's prayer of forgiveness on the cross. Forgiveness is a key tenet of the message Jesus would instruct His followers to proclaim in His name to all nations following His resurrection. Jesus's death proved His ministry of reconciliation, hope, and healing to be the truth.

H

E

A

R

T

DID YOU KNOW?
Don't miss this small detail in Matthew's account of Jesus's crucifixion—the faithful women stayed by Jesus's side to the end (27:55-56). "These women were the last at the cross and the first at the tomb (cf. Matt. 28:1) indicating their devotion to Jesus whom they had followed in Galilee and ministered to financially (Luke 8:2-3)."[15]

MEMORY VERSE
Continue practicing the memory verse you chose. Write out as much of it as you can from memory, and then check to see how you did.

MEMORY VERSES: LUKE 23:34; JOHN 17:3

WEEK IN REVIEW
Spend some time reflecting on what you have learned this week. Record a truth from each day that you want to remember, or go back and highlight portions of your journal.

DAY 1:

DAY 2:

DAY 3:

DAY 4:

DAY 5:

In chapter 18 John described Jesus's arrest and trials before the high priest and before Pilate. Pilate found no basis for the charges brought against Jesus, but he was unwilling to sacrifice himself and his own political interests to set Christ free. Therefore, he caved in to the religious leaders' demands for Jesus's death. Though Pilate handed Jesus over to the Jews to be crucified, it is important to note that Jesus willingly gave Himself to die a sacrificial death for the sins of the world. He gave Himself so that we could receive salvation through Him. Jesus's death occurred at the season of the Passover celebration. He died as the Lamb of God (John 1:29,36). The blood of the lambs sprinkled on their homes in obedience to God's command had spared the Israelites when the destroyer invaded the land of Egypt before the Israelites left for the promised land (Ex. 12:13). John wrote in 1 John 1:7 that "the blood of Jesus his Son cleanses us from all sin." Jesus died for us.

H

E

A

R

T

DAY 181 | MARK 16

MEMORY VERSES: MATTHEW 28:18-20; ACTS 1:8

All of Scripture points to the work and mission of Jesus, which seemed to have ended the day He hung on the cross at Calvary. At least that's how things appeared to His disciples who watched their promised Messiah die. Little did they know the cross was only part one of Jesus's redemptive act. With His death on the cross, Jesus paid God's penalty for the sins of the world, sins that required a blood sacrifice to purify sinners. Jesus did not remain in the grave. On the third day He rose from the dead and defeated death—the ultimate consequence of sin. Mark's Gospel documents the moment when three of Jesus's faithful followers, all women, showed up at His tomb to anoint His body. There they encountered an angel who told them the news of Jesus's resurrection. The angel also told them to take this news to the disciples and Peter. These same disciples deserted Jesus at the cross. God wanted this great news conveyed as an offer of restoration and forgiveness. Through the cross and resurrection of Jesus, God made a way for you—a sinful and broken daughter—to be reunited with Him as the recipient of His forgiveness and grace.

H

E

A

R

T

WEEK AT A GLANCE

As Psalm 30:5 says, "Weeping may stay overnight, but there is joy in the morning." That is what I feel as we start this week and celebrate Jesus's resurrection in our reading. I hope you are excited to dig in!

DAY 182 | LUKE 24

MEMORY VERSES: MATTHEW 28:18-20; ACTS 1:8

DAILY CHALLENGE

Think about a person who played a key role in helping you come to understand the gospel. If you have a way to contact that person, do that this week and let him or her know how his or her faithfulness to the gospel changed your life.

The Gospel of Luke also records the account of Jesus's resurrection and the women's faithful obedience in relaying the angel's message to the rest of the disciples. Luke also gives us details into Jesus's postresurrection appearances. Jesus's appearances proved His resurrection and provided Him the opportunity to give final charges to His disciples before ascending to heaven. Jesus appeared to two disciples on the road to Emmaus, when He also confirmed that all of Scripture points to Himself. Jesus later appeared to the apostles and showed them His hands and feet. He prompted them to believe the resurrection by eating with them and interpreting the Old Testament in light of His sufferings and resurrection. Jesus identified Himself as the Messiah. His time on earth ended with a commission to His disciples. He left them with the charge to minister and proclaim the gospel on His behalf. As Jesus's disciples today, we know Him because others have been faithful to carry His gospel around the world, and we pick up where those disciples left off as Jesus's faithful ambassadors.

H

E

A

R

T

MEMORY VERSE

Pick one of the memory verse options for this week—Matthew 28:18-20; Acts 1:8—and write the verse.

DAY 183 | JOHN 20-21

MEMORY VERSES: MATTHEW 28:18-20; ACTS 1:8

In John's Gospel account of Jesus's resurrection, John zooms in on specific conversations Jesus had with His disciples after His resurrection. We see how their faith was impacted by His resurrection, and as a result, how ours should be too. The evening after Mary discovered the empty tomb, Jesus appeared to His disciples who were huddled behind locked doors. Jesus appeared a week later to the disciples, including Thomas, who had a difficult time believing the news since he was absent during Jesus's first encounter. Jesus invited Thomas to see and touch His scars. Thomas responded in faith without touching His wounds. Jesus's final appearance was to Peter and six other disciples on the seashore as they were fishing. During that time, Jesus commissioned Peter to follow Him and minister to His people. Jesus's conversation with Peter demonstrates that love was essential for being a faithful disciple. Believers exemplify love for Jesus by caring for His people. If we really love Jesus, then we will serve Him by caring for other believers.

THINK ABOUT IT

Mary Magdalene discovered the empty tomb, was the first person the resurrected Jesus appeared to, and delivered the news of His resurrection to the rest of the disciples. Again we are reminded that God uses women to spread His Word and be His witnesses.

H

E

A

R

T

MEMORY VERSES: MATTHEW 28:18-20; ACTS 1:8

THINK ABOUT IT

"Go, therefore, and make disciples of all nations, baptizing them in the name of the Father and of the Son and of the Holy Spirit, teaching them to observe everything I have commanded you. And remember, I am with you always, to the end of the age'"

—Matthew 28:19-20

Have you taken the Great Commission seriously by making disciples? Whom are you investing in? Who is investing in you?

MEMORY VERSE

Continue practicing the memory verse you chose. Write out as much of it as you can from memory, and then check to see how you did.

The record of the resurrection is surprisingly short in all of the Gospels. The writers were not necessarily trying to prove the resurrection because it was considered largely indisputable in the early church. They were satisfied with sharing only a few of His appearances. What Matthew recorded is particularly significant for the assignment Jesus has given to all of His disciples throughout history. Matthew included Jesus's appearance to the women who found the empty tomb and His appearance to the eleven remaining disciples. It was then that Jesus gave the Great Commission, His command for the disciples to replicate the gospel ministry by making disciples. Sharing Christ and bringing people fully under God's reign is an ongoing lifestyle commitment, and one that should be lived out with the same sense of urgency the first disciples had. As we continue to live out the Great Commission today, we must remember we are not working in our own strength. Our task is not to be clever, motivational, or exciting. We are to be obedient—humbly claiming the promise that Jesus is with us always.

H

E

A

R

T

DAY 185 | ACTS 1

MEMORY VERSES: MATTHEW 28:18-20; ACTS 1:8

The book of Acts, written by the Gospel writer Luke, documents the early church during the first three decades after Jesus's ascension. Throughout those years, Christianity, which was first extended to the Jewish people, became predominantly Gentile. Acts 1 sets the stage for the coming of the Holy Spirit, which is described in Acts 2, by moving readers from Jesus's postresurrection appearances to the disciples prayerfully waiting in the upper room. Luke recorded Jesus's instructions to the disciples concerning their global mission, a task that would be aided by the Holy Spirit. Luke also includes the account of Jesus's ascension to heaven as the disciples watched. As Jesus prepared to leave, He gave the disciples a new perspective about the kingdom when He established a worldwide scope for this witnessing mission. The church, under the Holy Spirit's guidance and power, was to take the gospel to the ends of the earth, a task we are charged with continuing to carry out today.

H

E

A

R

T

WEEK IN REVIEW
Spend some time reflecting on what you have learned this week. Record a truth from each day that you want to remember, or go back and highlight portions of your journal.

DAY 1:

DAY 2:

DAY 3:

DAY 4:

DAY 5:

DAY 186 | ACTS 2–3

MEMORY VERSES: ACTS 2:42; ACTS 4:31

Exactly as Jesus had promised, the Father empowered the disciples with the Holy Spirit. We have been commissioned to witness about Christ's saving power to the uttermost parts of the earth and are dependent on the Spirit's power to accomplish this task. Chapter 2 ends with the crowd's response to Peter's sermon. Having come under conviction by the Holy Spirit, the people inquire about how to respond. Peter directs them to confess and repent of their sins. Chapters 2–3 provide a picture of the early church in action. Unity, generous giving, sharing with those in need, witnessing, worshiping, partaking of the Lord's Supper in fellowship, and serving the Lord through various ministries present a model for ministry. Modeled after Jesus's example, the disciples met people's physical and spiritual needs, both within and outside of the body of Christ. Just as He did in the first century, God continues to empower His people to meet the spiritual and physical needs of others in order that His name would be glorified and people would be drawn to Him.

WEEK AT A GLANCE

With last week's readings we finished the Gospels and now are moving on to the book of Acts. We're going to be in Acts all week, and we'll read about the coming of the Holy Spirit, the start of the church and a radical salvation testimony. However, opposition to Jesus was still rampant, and we'll read about the first Christian martyr as well. Before you begin reading, pray that the Lord will open your eyes to His truth this week.

H

E

A

R

T

DAY 187 | ACTS 4-5

MEMORY VERSES: ACTS 2:42; ACTS 4:31

The early church experienced many miraculous signs and wonders as a result of their unity with others and dependence upon the Spirit. Acts 4:32-37 describes how early believers shared their possessions for the purpose of meeting physical needs. Barnabas exemplified voluntary sharing among the believers. Sadly, not every member possessed pure motives. Ananias and Sapphira were dishonest about their personal contribution and, as a result, experienced the harsh judgment of death. Ananias and Sapphira remind us that the church is made up of imperfect people trying to meet the needs of others and bring people to Jesus. This is why a reliance on the wisdom and guidance of the Holy Spirit in daily life is vitally important. When we deviate from the leading of the Spirit, we are tempted to imitate the actions of Ananias and Sapphira, who misled the disciples with their offering. Because God is always about the business of accomplishing His good plans in our world, this event served to enhance the church's public ministry. People were encouraged to seek out the church's assistance, which led to conversations about the One who could satisfy every need.

H

E

A

R

T

THINK ABOUT IT
It's never easy to read about the discipline of the Lord, but like any good father, discipline is an important part of His relationship with His children. Reflect on these questions today:

What are some ways you've experienced the discipline of your heavenly Father?

How has your faith been refined through such an experience?

MEMORY VERSE
Pick one of the memory verse options for this week—Acts 2:42; Acts 4:31—and write the verse.

DAY 188 | ACTS 6

MEMORY VERSES: ACTS 2:42; ACTS 4:31

As the church continued to grow at a rapid pace, noticeable growing pains began to surface. In chapter 6 Luke described how some widows in the Christian community in Jerusalem were not receiving their daily distribution of food. This brought to the church's attention the need for better administration of service so the apostles could focus on the spread of the gospel. The church set apart seven men to head up this new ministry. As the gospel went forth, opposition against the church increased. Stephen, one of the seven men appointed to serve the widows, drew attention from the corrupt religious leaders because of his fearless proclamation of the Word of Christ. His preaching led some unbelieving Grecian Jews to bring him before the Sanhedrin on trumped-up charges. When the gospel changes lives through a noticeable impact on a community, opposition will arise. All who desire to live out Jesus's Great Commission in their lives can expect hardship and trouble along the way. However, God's Spirit will give you, like Stephen, the boldness and confidence to stand strong for Him.

H

E

A

R

T

DAY 189 | ACTS 7

MEMORY VERSES: ACTS 2:42; ACTS 4:31

In Acts 7 Luke recorded the defense Stephen gave before the Sanhedrin—a powerful testimony of the gospel, traced throughout the Old Testament. Stephen opened with God's calling of Abraham in Mesopotamia. He then highlighted Joseph and his brothers residing in Egypt. Next Stephen recounted the Israelites' slavery in Egypt and Moses's journey to freedom through the desert. He reminded the crowd of the Israelites' rebellion in the wilderness and how they worshiped an idol. After discussing the traveling tabernacle and the temple of Solomon, Stephen emphasized that God does not dwell in buildings. Stephen boldly warned the religious leaders about resisting the Holy Spirit. Their ancestors had persecuted and killed the prophets, and now the religious leaders had killed the Righteous One (Jesus), whom the prophets foretold. Stephen's defense was a powerful witness about Christ, which resulted in his death by stoning. He is the first martyr in the New Testament.

DID YOU KNOW?

Stephen's name means "crown." He was the first Christian to die specifically for his faith. Stephen "took seriously the commission of Jesus to carry the gospel to the whole world and led to the founding of the world mission movement that took the gospel to the whole Roman Empire in the first century."[16] What a legacy he left!

MEMORY VERSE

Continue practicing the memory verse you chose. Write out as much of it as you can from memory, and then check to see how you did.

H

E

A

R

T

MEMORY VERSES: ACTS 2:42; ACTS 4:31

WEEK IN REVIEW

Spend some time reflecting on what you have learned this week. Record a truth from each day that you want to remember, or go back and highlight portions of your journal.

DAY 1:

DAY 2:

DAY 3:

DAY 4:

DAY 5:

Stephen's stoning unleashed a persecution on the Jerusalem church that forced believers to flee from Jerusalem. Instead of extinguishing the gospel message, it expanded it. Saul, a persecutor of Christians, who later became known as the apostle Paul, is introduced at the account of Stephen's death. The chapter ends with Philip's one-on-one ministry to the Ethiopian eunuch, highlighting another conversation that reveals God's redemptive plan throughout all of Scripture. Chapter 9 begins with Saul's journey to exterminate all believers of Jesus in the city of Damascus. On the way to that city, Jesus encountered him, causing him to lose his sight. After meeting Ananias in Damascus, the former persecutor regained his sight, was filled with the Holy Spirit, and was eventually baptized. Almost immediately Paul began proclaiming the gospel. Few encounters in Scripture provide such a powerful picture of the immediate change Jesus brings to a person's life. If you are a Christian, then like Saul, you have a powerful testimony of how you have been raised from spiritual death to life through the good news of Christ. Don't ever take that story for granted.

H

E

A

R

T

DAY 191 | ACTS 10–11

MEMORY VERSES: JAMES 1:2-4; JAMES 2:17

Chapters 2–12 in the book of Acts largely focus on Peter's ministry. Through Peter's efforts, people understood that the gospel of Jesus Christ is a message for the whole world, not just for the Jews. In large part this revelation took place as a result of Peter's interactions with Cornelius, a Roman centurion in Caesarea who had a vision in which an angel told him to send men to Joppa to summon Peter. Meanwhile, Peter had a vision in which God commanded him to kill and eat animals that Jews considered unclean. When Cornelius's men arrived, the Spirit instructed Peter to accompany them to Caesarea. When he entered Cornelius's house, Peter shared how God had sent him and explained the truth he had learned about not considering anyone common or unclean. Peter preached the gospel to the people at Cornelius's house, the Spirit descended on the hearers, and they were baptized. The lesson for Peter and for all Christians today is that in God's kingdom, people are more important than religious regulations or racial differences. All people matter to God, and His desire is for all people to hear His gospel and experience the salvation it offers.

H

E

A

R

T

WEEK AT A GLANCE
This week we'll be reading in Acts about Peter's ministry and Paul being set apart for the mission field. We'll finish this week by reading the book of James. At this point you only have thirteen weeks left of reading through *The Bible in a Year.* Keep it up!

DAY 192 | ACTS 12

MEMORY VERSES: JAMES 1:2-4; JAMES 2:17

THINK ABOUT IT

"The world was made partly that there may be prayer; partly that our prayers might be answered."[17]

–C. S. Lewis

Think about your own prayer life. How can you alter your schedule and priorities this week to make prayer a more consistent aspect of your day-to-day life?

MEMORY VERSE

Pick one of the memory verse options for this week—James 1:2-4; James 2:17—and write the verse.

Persecutions against the early church continued, even though Paul was no longer leading the charge. King Herod Agrippa I, the ruler of Judea, beheaded the apostle James and imprisoned Peter. Acts 12 described how an angel miraculously freed Peter from prison. Herod discovered that Peter had escaped, had Peter's guards executed, and journeyed to Caesarea. There Herod suffered a horrible death. In spite of the oppression, the gospel continued to flourish. Additionally, Barnabas and Paul completed their relief mission at this time. It's easy to overlook a small detail in Acts 12:5. While Peter was in prison, the church earnestly prayed for him, likely for his safety and strength in the face of persecution. The events that followed show the power of their prayers, which reminds us that prayer is the most effective tool we have against any opposition or temptation we face, both in our personal lives and as the church today. Through prayer we commune with God and rely on Him for every aspect of our lives.

H

E

A

R

T

DAY 193 | ACTS 13–14

MEMORY VERSES: JAMES 1:2-4; JAMES 2:17

With Acts 13 Luke shifted his focus from Peter to Paul. One of the consistent themes of Paul's missionary efforts was preaching in the synagogue, which he did several times in Acts 13–14. Paul was born and raised as a devout Jew, and conversion of the Jews was at the heart of his ministry. However, most Jews were not receptive to Paul's gospel message; therefore, he took the message to the Gentiles. Paul's preaching always included that Jesus was the Son of God, who was crucified, raised from death, and the means through which people can receive forgiveness of sins and be made right with God. This message stirred people's hearts both to belief and to anger. Those Paul angered often tried to kill him, as is evident from Acts 13–14, though these threats on his life never hindered Paul's witness. Through Paul's example, we are reminded that serving Christ brings with it both highs and lows. Regardless of what we encounter as we live for Christ, God expects us to be faithful to the task He has given us.

DID YOU KNOW?

Three of Paul's missionary journeys are recorded in the book of Acts. On his first journey (Acts 13:1–14:28), Paul traveled to Cyprus, Perga, Pisidian Antioch, Iconium, Lystra, and Derbe.

H

E

A

R

T

DAY 194 | JAMES 1-2

MEMORY VERSES: JAMES 1:2-4; JAMES 2:17

THINK ABOUT IT

Among the many things we learn from the beginning of James's letter is the truth that a believer must be a hearer and doer of the Word of God. How can you go from a hearer this week to a doer of the Word?

Acts 12:17 identified James, the brother of Jesus, as a leader of the church in Jerusalem. The book of James is a practical book that addresses issues Christians deal with both within and outside of the church. In chapter 1 James reminded his readers that God offers believers wisdom to cope with times of trials and testing. He pointed out that God never tempts anyone; temptations arise from people's sin natures. God, on the other hand, graciously gives only good gifts to those He loves. James also emphasized the importance of listening to and obeying the Word of God. By applying God's Word, we give evidence that our religion is genuine. Application of the Word involves controlling speech, caring for needy people, and maintaining purity of life. In chapter 2 James shifted his focus from religion to personal faith. As Christians, we are obligated to love others. We are sinning when we fail to do so. Love is one of the ways we put feet to our faith, which, as James pointed out, is dead without actions. The point James makes in these two chapters is that saving faith in Jesus changes a person from the inside out.

H

E

A

R

T

MEMORY VERSE

Continue practicing the memory verse you chose. Write out as much of it as you can from memory, and then check to see how you did.

DAY 195 | JAMES 3–5

MEMORY VERSES: JAMES 1:2-4; JAMES 2:17

One of the running themes throughout James's letter is right Christian behavior. As people transformed by Jesus, Christians are to live and act differently than the rest of the world. Paul specifically connected this to speech. James emphasized the power of our words—either for good or for bad—and the need for consistency in believers' speech. James also reminded his readers that Christians must rely on the wisdom of God to control their behavior. In addition to speech, James also warned against the danger of unaddressed conflict. Evidently, judging others was a significant problem in the early church, which fueled conflicts. James stressed the availability of God's grace to correct believers' conflicts with one another. On the basis of that grace, he called on them to submit and draw near to God through repentance and humility. After some additional teachings, James closed his letter by calling for believers to be patient through suffering as they await Jesus's return and to endure on the basis of God's nature. In the meantime, we are to maintain our faith in God and utilize the power of prayer He has given us.

H

E

A

R

T

DAY 196 | ACTS 15–16

MEMORY VERSES: ACTS 17:11; ACTS 17:24-25

As the church continued to grow, so did the need for clarity between Jewish and Christian beliefs and practices. Paul and Barnabas met with the council at Jerusalem to shore up some discrepancies over the role of circumcision and the Old Testament law in the life of new covenant believers. Peter declared that Jews were saved by grace, just as Gentiles were. Paul, Barnabas, and James also affirmed God's intention that Gentiles be included in His chosen family. Following this council, Paul set out on his second missionary journey, and at this point, Barnabas and Paul parted ways because of an issue with John Mark. In response to a vision, Paul traveled to Philippi with Silas, where Lydia and her household became believers. Paul's exorcising a fortune-telling spirit from a slave girl resulted in the missionaries' imprisonment. An earthquake opened the jail's doors, but none of the prisoners escaped. Paul and Silas shared Christ with the jailer, and he and his household became believers. Because of Paul's Roman citizenship, the missionaries were freed and resumed their journey.

H

E

A

WEEK AT A GLANCE
This week we'll be reading in Acts about the time in Paul's ministry when he met a disciple named Timothy. We'll also read Paul's letter to the Galatians.

R

T

DAY 197 | GALATIANS 1-3

As with many of his New Testament letters, Paul wrote his letter to the Galatians with a specific purpose and audience in mind. He wrote Galatians to correct their faulty understanding of faith and practice related to the gospel. Like the issue raised at the Jerusalem Council, many in Galatia were Judaizers, which means they falsely believed Gentiles had to be converted to Judaism in order to be Christians. However, as Paul argued in his letter, that belief flies in the face of the freedom from bondage to the law that is at the heart of Jesus's gospel. Paul emphasized that justification (being made right before God) comes by grace through faith in Christ, not through keeping the law. Paul contrasted living under the law to living by faith. The law fulfilled its purpose in that it acted as a guardian to God's people, protecting them as a foreshadowing or representation of the covering blood of Christ that was to come. It was also a guide to the coming Messiah. When Christ did come, He fulfilled the law, which means faith in Him is the only requirement to experience His saving faith. Obedience to God's law follows as the way we live out our faith in Him.

H

E

A

R

T

DAILY CHALLENGE

After completing your reading and journaling for today, reflect on this question:

Despite Jesus's work to free us from bondage to the law, we often struggle with trying to earn God's love and grace. What can you do this week to intentionally live in light of the gospel's grace instead of your own works?

MEMORY VERSE

Pick one of the memory verse options for this week—Acts 17:11; Acts 17:24-25—and write the verse.

MEMORY VERSES: ACTS 17:11; ACTS 17:24-25

DAILY CHALLENGE

Galatians 5:16-26 teaches us that the Holy Spirit produces fruit in the life of a believer. This fruit is the evidence of a person belonging to Jesus. This fruit includes the Christlike attributes of:

- love
- joy
- peace
- patience
- kindness
- goodness
- faithfulness
- gentleness
- self-control

Circle the traits on this list that need extra attention and prayer from you today. Ask God to grow those traits in you.

In Galatians 4–6 Paul emphasized the Christian's identity as a redeemed child of God and one's freedom from that understanding. God has adopted believers as His children and given them the Holy Spirit. They are no longer slaves but heirs of God, which is why it's offensive to God when we obey the law in an attempt to earn His love and grace. Paul emphasized that God's call to salvation in Christ is a call to freedom. This freedom is not license to sin but liberation to serve others. Loving others fulfills the law. Infighting among Christians, however, is destructive, as is any item on the list of the works of the flesh, which Paul mentioned in chapter 5. Conversely, the Spirit's activity in Christians produces a cluster of virtues—the fruit of the Spirit—which provides evidence that a person belongs to Christ. As those in Christ, we have the responsibility to help bear one another's burdens and do good to others. The point Paul makes repeatedly in Galatians is that true spiritual transformation only comes through the gospel.

H

E

A

R

T

DAY 199 | ACTS 17–18:17

MEMORY VERSES: ACTS 17:11; ACTS 17:24-25

Acts 17 documents Paul's ministry in Thessalonica, a place where the gospel was well received. Not surprisingly, jealous Jews forced them on to Berea, where many accepted their message of Christ. Again Jews from Thessalonica caused trouble, so Paul embarked on a journey to Athens. During his stay he presented the gospel to Jews and Gentiles, some of whom put their faith in Jesus. From Athens Paul traveled to Corinth, where he befriended Priscilla and Aquila, who made a living as tentmakers. When Jews in the synagogue rejected him, he took the message to the Gentiles. For eighteen months Paul taught the Word of God in a house. Antagonistic Jews accused Paul of breaking the law, but Gallio, the proconsul, dismissed the charges. From this time in Paul's ministry, God's hand was on him; his commitment to the gospel was evidence of this fact. Like Paul, we need to trust God's leadership in our lives as we live out the calling He has given us to go and make disciples.

DID YOU KNOW?
Paul's second missionary journey is recorded in Acts 15:36–18:22. He traveled to Syria, Cilicia, Derbe, Lystra, Phrygia, Galatia, Troas, Philippi, Thessalonica, Berea, Athens, Corinth, Ephesus, Caesarea, Jerusalem, and Antioch.

MEMORY VERSE
Continue practicing the memory verse you chose. Write out as much of it as you can from memory, and then check to see how you did.

H

E

A

R

T

DAY 200 | 1 THESSALONIANS 1-2

MEMORY VERSES: ACTS 17:11; ACTS 17:24-25

WEEK IN REVIEW
Spend some time reflecting on what you have learned this week. Record a truth from each day that you want to remember, or go back and highlight portions of your journal.

DAY 1:

During his time in Thessalonica, Paul formed a strong bond with the Christians there. The new believers had embraced the gospel enthusiastically and formed a church, but because of Paul's abrupt departure, the believers were immature in the faith. However, Paul reminded them of key events in their lives as believers. Paul thanked God for the transformation he witnessed in their lives as a result of embracing the gospel. They were outstanding examples for other Christians, both near and far. In chapter 2 Paul reminded them about the purpose of his ministry while he lived among them. We look to the apostle Paul as the foremost example of what Christians are to believe and how we are to behave as we seek to grow in Christlikeness. Throughout his life and ministry, Paul placed an emphasis on loving others and sharing the gospel boldly. As Paul demonstrated, we are to live in such a way that both our words and actions draw people to the saving grace and transforming love of God.

DAY 2:

H

DAY 3:

E

DAY 4:

A

DAY 5:

R

T

DAY 201 | 1 THESSALONIANS 3-5

MEMORY VERSES: 1 CORINTHIANS 1:18;
1 THESSALONIANS 5:23-24

Paul devoted the first half of his letter to compliment the Thessalonian Christians on their actions and remind them of his expectations for them. In chapter 3 he focuses on practical application of the gospel. Paul was concerned for the Thessalonians' present and future sanctification. Everything they did was to be driven by the overarching goal of pleasing God in daily living. These instructions also included teaching about Jesus's second coming. We all have unanswerable questions about Jesus's return, but what is important to remember is that Jesus's promised return is to be a source of hope, comfort, and motivation for our present walk with Christ. While we wait, we are to be united with other believers in the church who are striving for Christlikeness with us. For believers, faith (toward God) and love (toward one another) are nothing new. These attitudes are to characterize the Christian life from the beginning. An ongoing challenge for twenty-first century believers is to show that we are living in anticipation of Jesus's return through behavior distinguished by love, faith, and hope.

H

E

A

R

T

> **WEEK AT A GLANCE**
> As Paul traveled on his missionary journeys, he wrote letters to area churches to encourage them and to address their struggles and growing pains. The church at Thessalonica and the church at Corinth received letters from Paul, which we'll read this week.

DAY 202 | 2 THESSALONIANS 1-3

MEMORY VERSES: 1 CORINTHIANS 1:18;
1 THESSALONIANS 5:23-24

DAILY CHALLENGE

Paul was adamant that believers need accountability and encouragement in their faith journey. Fill in the blanks below with the name of one person who currently plays that role in your life, and one person for whom you can offer that.

I am encouraged by:

_____

I am encouraging:

_____

MEMORY VERSE

Pick one of the memory verse options for this week—1 Corinthians 1:18; 1 Thessalonians 5:23-24— and write the verse.

Shortly after Paul had written and sent his first letter to this group of new believers, he received a report about issues confronting them, prompting him to send them a follow-up letter. Their questions were of Jesus's second coming, an event Paul had touched on briefly in his first letter. Paul instructed them to wait and watch for Jesus's return and not fall prey to false teachers around them. Each chapter of Paul's second letter emphasizes God's sovereignty in a variety of situations. Paul pointed them to God's justice, both now and in the future, which enables believers to feel safe despite troubling circumstances. Paul closed his letter to the church at Thessalonica by encouraging members to hold one another accountable and encourage one another in their pursuits of Jesus. We can endure together because God has proved His faithfulness to us through the life, death, and resurrection of Jesus. Through Jesus we can hold on to the promise God has given us of eternal life with Him.

H

E

A

R

T

DAY 203 | ACTS 18:18–19:41

MEMORY VERSES: 1 CORINTHIANS 1:18;
1 THESSALONIANS 5:23-24

After Paul's time in Thessalonica and Athens, he traveled on to Corinth and then later to Ephesus. In both cities he preached first in the Jewish synagogue until he was driven out at which point he directed his efforts to the Gentiles. Paul encountered serious opposition at Ephesus from the silversmiths of the city. Seeing Paul as a threat to their business (which focused largely on making idols), they enacted a riot in which they portrayed Paul as the archenemy of their city and the temple of Artemis. Paul could have been killed had it not been for the intervention of others. In order to remain true to the gospel, Paul witnessed of the only true God by revealing the foolishness of worshiping idols. Likewise, we should stand countercultural to our communities whenever its values run contrary to the truth of the Scriptures. When we speak out, we may become a disrupting presence and should expect conflict and criticism. Only when we are willing to risk our pride and reputation will we really be able to make a difference in our world.

DID YOU KNOW?
Paul's third missionary journey is recorded in Acts 18:23–21:26. He traveled to Galatia, Phrygia, Ephesus, Corinth, Macedonia, Greece, Achaia, Troas, Miletus, Tyre, Ptolemais, Caesarea, and Jerusalem.

H

E

A

R

T

DAY 204 | 1 CORINTHIANS 1-2

MEMORY VERSES: 1 CORINTHIANS 1:18;
1 THESSALONIANS 5:23-24

DAILY CHALLENGE

"For who has known the Lord's mind, that he may instruct him? But we have the mind of Christ."

–1 Corinthians 2:16

When in your spiritual journey did the mind of Christ start to make a difference in your values, choices, and decisions?

What will you do differently today in light of what you have read and studied?

MEMORY VERSE

Continue practicing the memory verse you chose. Write out as much of it as you can from memory, and then check to see how you did.

During Paul's time in Ephesus, he received a troubling report about the state of the church in Corinth, so he wrote a letter to them, which is included in our canon of Scripture. One of the main issues facing this church was a lack of unity. Many teachers, some of whom presented different messages, visited the churches in the New Testament. As a result, various factions that favored one Christian leader over another threatened the unity of the church and undermined its effectiveness. Paul's solution was to focus the church's attention solely on Christ and His message, which includes the gift of the Holy Spirit and the wisdom He brings. People without Christ do not have the Holy Spirit to aid them in comprehending God's revealed truth, which is the reason they do not receive what comes from God's Spirit. However, those indwelled with the Spirit of the Lord have the mind of Christ. Although no human being can know everything about God, our understanding of Him and His purposes always has room to expand. God will give us the needed spiritual insight to understand more about Him through the Holy Spirit's involvement in our lives.

H

E

A

R

T

DAY 205 | 1 CORINTHIANS 3-4

MEMORY VERSES: 1 CORINTHIANS 1:18;
1 THESSALONIANS 5:23-24

The lack of unity in the Corinthian church proved to Paul that these Christians were still infants, or babies, in their spiritual maturity. This is why he focused much of his letter on instructing and reminding them about how to live and mature as followers of Christ in the church. This weakness among them highlighted the importance of the need for spiritual leaders in their church, something they were overlooking. Paul taught that church leaders serve God, and as a result, are accountable first and foremost to Him. Paul insisted that being an effective Christian leader included humbly enduring suffering for the faith, whether physically or through criticism. He sought to present the Corinthians with a servant image of leadership, one that followed Jesus's example. Leadership is a call to serve humbly, not to strut proudly. Above all, they must prove faithful. Paul claimed that all leaders should be evaluated only by the standard of fidelity to Christ, not by eloquence and pretentious human wisdom. When we recognize our accountability to God and pursue His agenda rather than our own, the result will be unity within the church.

H

E

A

R

T

DAY 206 | 1 CORINTHIANS 5-6

MEMORY VERSES: 1 CORINTHIANS 10:13; 1 CORINTHIANS 13:13

Paul's letters to the Corinthians explain how the body of believers was desperately in need of spiritual growth and godly leadership. Paul was stunned by an incident of immorality in the church involving a man's inappropriate sexual misconduct with his stepmother. Apparently, the church turned a blind eye toward this behavior. Paul severely rebuked both the man and the church. The church's role in the matter was not only to express displeasure with the man's behavior but also to actively seek to change his behavior. In 1 Corinthians 6:1-11 Paul further emphasized the church's responsibility to live morally by addressing the matter of lawsuits between believers. The Corinthian church members needed to embrace Christian ethics completely and to reject any immoral conduct in their fellowship. Paul closed this section with a reminder that Christian freedom is not a license to do anything we want but rather a freedom to embrace Christian morality as God intended. On both a personal and corporate level, reflecting on Christ's work of forgiveness and reconciliation in our lives reminds us of our need to repent of sins and rely on His grace.

H

WEEK AT A GLANCE

This week the entirety of our time will be spent reading in 1 Corinthians. Paul will teach on several topics, including sexual misconduct, singleness, marriage, idols, church conduct, spiritual gifts, and the resurrection. We'll cover a lot of ground, so let's get started!

E

A

R

T

DAY 207 | 1 CORINTHIANS 7

Generally speaking, the first six chapters of 1 Corinthians are Paul's response to a report he had received with some alarming revelations about the conduct of some church members in Corinth. After dealing with these matters, Paul shifted to dealing with questions the Corinthians had raised in a letter to him. The Corinthians' first question concerned marriage and sexuality. Having addressed sexual immorality in chapters 5–6, Paul moved to address a related question from their letter. His topics in chapter 7 are abstinence, conduct within a marriage, grateful acceptance of the life to which God calls each person, and potential blessings of singleness. Whether married or single, every Christian should be a slave of Christ. We are to live surrendered to Jesus and the spread of His gospel. One of the great paradoxes in the Christian faith is that only through submission to Christ do we find true freedom. This is a recurring theme in Paul's letters. Living for God is more important than everything else in life.

H

E

A

R

T

DAILY CHALLENGE

After reading today's text and journaling your response, consider the following questions:

How divided is your devotion to the Lord in your current season of life?

What are the main things that are distracting you?

What is one step you can take to minimize distractions this week?

MEMORY VERSE

Pick one of the memory verse options for this week— 1 Corinthians 10:13; 1 Corinthians 13:13— and write the verse.

DAY 208 | 1 CORINTHIANS 8–9

MEMORY VERSES: 1 CORINTHIANS 10:13; 1 CORINTHIANS 13:13

DAILY CHALLENGE

In this passage you see Paul's deep passion for sharing the gospel. List the names of five people in your circles of influence who need to hear the good news of Jesus from you:

1.

2.

3.

4.

5.

The city of Corinth was known for its immorality and perversion, which created a challenging atmosphere for new Christians to live out their faith and its counter cultural practices. To compound the problems, many of the Corinthian Christians were impressed with their own knowledge and spirituality. This pride led to insensitivity in their relationships with other Christians and inappropriate conduct. Paul addressed some of their questions about behavior in chapters 8–9. The first matter Paul addressed concerned whether Christians should eat food that had been offered to idols. Although Paul agreed with those who asserted that idols are nothing, he reminded them that Christians also need to consider how their actions might impact other believers who don't share their same conviction. Christians show maturity when they avoid behavior that isn't inherently sinful but still might hinder another believer's spiritual growth. In 9:1-27 Paul used himself as an example of this principle. He didn't want any of his actions to hinder him in sharing the gospel. Paul regularly emphasized his goal of reaching people for Christ and leading them to a more focused discipleship. For him, that mission trumped every other consideration.

H

E

A

R

T

DAY 209 | 1 CORINTHIANS 10–11

MEMORY VERSES: 1 CORINTHIANS 10:13; 1 CORINTHIANS 13:13

In 1 Corinthians 10:1-11 Paul returned to the issue of food that had been offered to idols. He did so in the context of helping his readers better understand Christian freedom. As Christians, his readers had an obligation to resist all forms of temptation. Paul urged mature Christians to embrace the responsibility of seeking what was good for other believers over insisting they were free in Christ to engage in certain activities. Paul also addressed the matter of proper conduct in worship. Specific questions concerned head coverings, fellowship meals, and the Lord's Supper. The problems concerning these issues revolved around selfish behavior that was inconsistent with the holy lives they were called to lead. With freedom in Christ comes great responsibility. As new creations in Christ, we need to choose things that further God's kingdom and mission over things that hold us back. This means allowing someone else to rule and lead our lives and requires us to abandon our will and control. Following Christ gives us a desire to change our ways and a desire for the gospel to be known.

H

E

A

R

T

WEEK IN REVIEW

Spend some time reflecting on what you have learned this week. Record a truth from each day that you want to remember, or go back and highlight portions of your journal.

DAY 1:

DAY 2:

DAY 3:

DAY 4:

DAY 5:

DAY 210 | 1 CORINTHIANS 12–14

MEMORY VERSES: 1 CORINTHIANS 10:13; 1 CORINTHIANS 13:13

Among the many problems the Corinthian church faced, one thorny issue centered on the nature and purpose of spiritual gifts. Some church members viewed the type of gift a believer possessed as a measuring stick for that believer's level of spirituality. In response to this issue, Paul set out a basic rule for consideration of all spiritual gifts: all Christians share the common confession of faith that Jesus is Lord. On this foundation Paul affirmed the value of spiritual gifts and insisted they were not a criterion for ranking Christians. He listed various gifts and declared that each gift came from one and the same source—the Holy Spirit. Using the analogy of the body, Paul argued that every gift is necessary; therefore, every Christian is important. All gifts, no matter what purpose they serve in the church, must be governed by Christlike love, which he elaborated on in chapter 13. Without Christlike love as their motive, spiritual gifts are empty shells. Love expressed is the way church members then and today are to demonstrate they are the body of Christ on earth. Furthermore, Paul reminded them in chapter 14 that when the church gathers for worship, the purpose should always be to exalt God and strengthen all who are present.

H

E

A

R

T

DAY 211 | 1 CORINTHIANS 15–16

MEMORY VERSES: ROMANS 1:16-17; 1 CORINTHIANS 15:3-4

A chief purpose of 1 Corinthians was to answer questions and challenges from the Corinthian church, none of which were more pivotal than their questions about the resurrection. Some church members were questioning the resurrection. Apparently they didn't doubt Jesus's resurrection, but they failed to see how Jesus's resurrection was a guarantee that God would raise all believers. The natural connection between Jesus's resurrection and that of believers dovetails out of our union with Christ, a major theme throughout Paul's correspondence with the Corinthians. These verses describe the grand sweep of human history from the fall of Adam to the consummation of God's kingdom. Every Christ follower's story ends with resurrection and eternal communion with Christ, which reminds us that we are not to live only for the present day. Because our actions have eternal consequences, each day's choices are important. The future hope of being with Christ and being made new colors and shapes every aspect of our Christian life. We live for the greater cause in the present because everything we do for Christ matters eternally.

H

E

A

R

T

WEEK AT A GLANCE
Today we'll be reading the end of 1 Corinthians and go right into 2 Corinthians for the remainder of the week. Paul will address the resurrection of Jesus Christ as we close out 1 Corinthians. He then addresses hardships in ministry as we jump into 2 Corinthians.

DAY 212 | 2 CORINTHIANS 1–2

MEMORY VERSES: ROMANS 1:16-17; 1 CORINTHIANS 15:3-4

READ ON
Read 1 Peter 3:18;
Hebrews 2:9; and
Romans 8:34.

What do these verses
teach you about Jesus?

How do these truths
impact your faith in
God's promises, like
Paul taught on in
2 Corinthians 2?

MEMORY VERSE
Pick one of the memory
verse options for this
week—Romans 1:16-17;
1 Corinthians 15:3-4—
and write the verse.

Paul wrote a handful of letters to the church in Corinth, but only two of them made it into Scripture. The purpose of 2 Corinthians is to express Paul's joy in the good report he received about the church, to strengthen his ties with individual church members, to confront outsiders who were trying to undermine Paul's ministry at the church, and to encourage the Corinthian believers to refocus their efforts by participating in a relief offering. In 2 Corinthians 1–2 we witness the vital connection between Paul's commitment to Christ and his commitment to working out difficult relationships. One of the truths about God that we cannot miss from these chapters is that we serve a God who keeps His promises, something we have seen proved true throughout the entirety of Scripture. Paul described the promises of God as being yes in Christ. We know that God will keep His promises to us because He has proved Himself trustworthy through the life, death, and resurrection of Jesus Christ. He is the same yesterday, today, and for eternity. Because God keeps His promises, we can wait confidently for all of them to be fulfilled. With this confidence in God's promises, we are able to follow in Paul's footsteps of unrelenting commitment to the gospel.

H

E

A

R

T

DAY 213 | 2 CORINTHIANS 3-4

MEMORY VERSES: ROMANS 1:16-17; 1 CORINTHIANS 15:3-4

Although things were going well in Corinth, Paul did have some opponents there who were raising doubts about his message and motives. Paul responded to these opponents by reminding the Corinthians of his qualifications and his work among them. To prove his case, Paul highlighted all the suffering he had endured, and he contended that his suffering proved that ministry success rested in God's power, not human accomplishments. To help his readers understand, Paul used the imagery of jars of clay, which people in his day owned to hold their most valuable possessions. God has given His people the greatest treasure in the universe—the gospel of Jesus Christ. But believing in this treasure does not make us impervious to pain. Instead, we have this treasure in our clay-like lives. Just as people of the time had to shatter the clay jars in which they kept their valuables to reveal the treasure, so God must at times break His people for the gospel to shine forth. When a person is broken, Jesus shines through. God uses these breaking circumstances to bring Himself glory and mold us into His image.

READ ON

Paul was not the only person in Scripture to use the jars of clay imagery to represent human weakness. Read Psalm 31:12 and Isaiah 30:14. God's power works through us even (and sometimes especially) in our weaknesses and sufferings.

H

E

A

R

T

DAY 214 | 2 CORINTHIANS 5-6

MEMORY VERSES: ROMANS 1:16-17; 1 CORINTHIANS 15:3-4

DAILY CHALLENGE

As you read
2 Corinthians 6:16-18,
underline the promises
God made to His
children. Then circle
the commands He
gives them:

"For we are the temple of
the living God, as God
said: I will dwell and
walk among them, and
I will be their God, and
they will be my people.
Therefore, come out
from among them
and be separate, says
the Lord; do not touch
any unclean thing,
and I will welcome you.
And I will be a Father to
you, and you will be sons
and daughters to me,
says the Lord Almighty."

MEMORY VERSE

Continue practicing the
memory verse you chose.
Write out as much of it
as you can from memory,
and then check to see
how you did.

Because of the hardships Christians endure living for the gospel, which Paul described in chapter 4, it is important that we learn to set our eyes on eternity. Suffering because of Christ is preparation for eternity because it challenges us to faithfully serve God and live each day for our future with Him. While eternity holds the promise of hope for the Christian, it brings the promise of judgment and condemnation for those who do not know Jesus, which is why Paul also emphasized the importance of the ministry of reconciliation, both with God and with others. Paul's motivation for seeking reconciliation with others was God's love. Christ's love compelled him to continue loving and reaching out to the Corinthians, even when they wronged him. He couldn't accept reconciliation from God and then refuse to pursue reconciliation with other believers. As we recognize the true price for our sin, we should be more and more grateful for Jesus's willing sacrifice on our behalf. As we grow to understand our identity in Christ, we will embrace the great task with which God has blessed us in Christ—to be His ambassadors of Christ's message of reconciliation.

H

E

A

R

T

DAY 215 | 2 CORINTHIANS 7-8

MEMORY VERSES: ROMANS 1:16-17; 1 CORINTHIANS 15:3-4

Second Corinthians 7 provides additional insight into Paul's interaction with the church at Corinth. He had received a report from Titus concerning the church and rejoiced that their once-strained relationship was improving. Paul's goal throughout his long-distance relationship with Corinth was to maintain love and intimacy. Moving to more practical matters, Paul addressed the need for a relief offering for needy Christians in Jerusalem. Sacrificial generosity was a practice the church established at its very conception in Acts 2; therefore, Paul reminds the church that generosity should be fundamental in their ministry to one another. Paul told the Corinthians about the generosity of the Macedonian churches who—despite their own poverty—had raised money for the poor Christians in Jerusalem. Even though they were poor, they gave generously because the Christian community was in need. Second Corinthians 8:9 reveals what should motivate all believers to willingly sacrifice of themselves for the sake of others in the community—Jesus's sacrifice for us. Jesus practiced and taught sacrificial giving. Gratitude to Jesus motivates us to demonstrate responsible stewardship of our lives and our possessions.

H

E

A

R

T

DAY 1:

DAY 2:

DAY 3:

DAY 4:

DAY 5:

DAY 216 | 2 CORINTHIANS 9–10

MEMORY VERSES: 2 CORINTHIANS 10:4; ROMANS 5:1

Continuing the topic of giving from chapter 8, Paul challenged the Corinthians to give freely and cheerfully, not by compulsion, so their gift would be a blessing—not only to the recipients but to the givers as well. The same attitude should characterize our own acts of giving today. After reminding the Corinthians that giving in this matter would be a witness for the gospel to others, Paul switched his topic and tone. Paul aimed to confront directly certain people in the church who were undermining him and his ministry coworkers. He belonged to God, and his motives for serving God were pure. In defending himself and his teaching, Paul reminds his readers then and now that we are in the midst of a very real spiritual battle—one that takes place largely in our minds (10:2-5). In the battlefield of the mind, we must be on guard for and actively battle against wrong ways of thinking that can interfere with our personal growth in Christ and our witness for Him to the world. By calling us to take our thoughts captive, Paul reminds us that we must play an active role in aligning our thoughts with the things of Christ.

H

WEEK AT A GLANCE
This week we'll finish up 2 Corinthians and then head into Romans. Paul taught the Corinthian church about giving, about keeping watch for false teachers, and about God's grace being sufficient even in the midst of suffering. With Romans we'll set off on a whole new reading adventure, so let's get this week started!

E

A

R

T

DAY 217 | 2 CORINTHIANS 11–13

MEMORY VERSES: 2 CORINTHIANS 10:4; ROMANS 5:1

In the closing section of his letter, Paul conveyed his concerns about the Corinthians. Though reluctant to appear harsh, Paul refused to allow his critics to mischaracterize and undermine his Christian service. Rather than call attention to his knowledge, experience, and abilities, Paul cited all of his struggles as evidence of his integrity and devotion to Christ. Through all of these difficulties, which included a thorn in his flesh that God would not remove, Paul learned the life-changing truth that God's power is demonstrated in the midst of human weakness. Rather than removing Paul's suffering, God gave him something better—sufficient grace for Paul to rise above it by depending on God's power. Our own weaknesses open the door for God's power to flow through us, like Paul, changing not only our lives but also the lives of those we come in contact with. Paul closed his second letter to the Corinthians with the promise to visit them again, which further challenged them to pursue spiritual growth and maturity in Christ.

DAILY CHALLENGE

Reflect on a time when you felt God's strength in the midst of great human weakness. Write a poem or draw a picture that illustrates that season of your life and the impact it had on your relationship with the Lord.

MEMORY VERSE

Pick one of the memory verse options for this week— 2 Corinthians 10:4; Romans 5:1—and write the verse.

H

E

A

R

T

MEMORY VERSES: 2 CORINTHIANS 10:4; ROMANS 5:1

DAILY CHALLENGE

The opening of Romans presents a striking picture of our need for God's grace. Underline all of the words or phrases in Romans 1–2 that describe who you are apart from Christ. Now circle all of the words or phrases that describe God's character and His work to draw you to Him in repentance. What is your takeaway from this exercise?

During Paul's third missionary journey he spent time in Greece, at which time he wrote his letter to the Romans. Paul's plan was to make his way to Rome, so he wrote this letter to the Christians there in order to communicate his life calling and the message he longed to tell others. Paul was writing to proclaim the gospel, a message built on the foundation of the Old Testament and fulfilled in Jesus Christ. To establish the universal need for the gospel, Paul pointed to the undeniable presence of sin in our world and our lives. At its core sin is idolatry—the worship of the creation instead of the Creator. Paul declared that God will render His judgment on those whose hearts are unrepentant. On the other hand, He will give eternal life to those who show by their actions that they have His law written on their hearts. Paul's main point is this: until we realize we are sinners by nature, we won't realize our desperate need for salvation and appreciate God's grace.

H

E

A

R

T

DAY 219 | ROMANS 3-4

MEMORY VERSES: 2 CORINTHIANS 10:4; ROMANS 5:1

Paul spent a good portion of Romans helping the Jews understand how they needed God's grace as much as Gentiles (non-Jews) do. The truth that all people stand condemned for sin means that Jews and Gentiles are equally guilty before God. No one can be justified by the works of the law, which is why everyone needs Jesus. Only by grace through faith in Him can a person experience salvation. Paul reminded his Jewish readers that the covenant promises God made to Abraham and his descendants were assured by faith, not by the law. God's promises were a display of grace to Abraham and to all who respond to God with faith like Abraham's, faith that trusts God to give life to the dead and to call things into existence that do not exist. For Paul, such an example as Abraham's was proof that the gospel of Jesus Christ both continued and fulfilled what had always been God's plan of salvation. Those who come to God by placing their faith in Jesus will find they are forgiven of sins and have been made right with God.

H

E

A

R

T

DAILY CHALLENGE

The gospel is the clearest picture we have of God's promise-keeping nature. Using Romans 3:23-25, write your own summary of the gospel's message and reflect on that truth throughout the week.

MEMORY VERSE

Continue practicing the memory verse you chose. Write out as much of it as you can from memory, and then check to see how you did.

DAY 220 | ROMANS 5-6

MEMORY VERSES: 2 CORINTHIANS 10:4; ROMANS 5:1

WEEK IN REVIEW

Spend some time reflecting on what you have learned this week. Record a truth from each day that you want to remember, or go back and highlight portions of your journal.

DAY 1:

DAY 2:

DAY 3:

DAY 4:

DAY 5:

Paul began Romans 5 by focusing on the present benefits of peace, hope, and love from God, all benefits that a believer can count on every day. God doesn't save us by grace only to make us then try to live for Him in our own power. God's grace is given to help us stand today, tomorrow, and on that future day when we will stand before His throne. Paul also described how God redeemed us when we were at our worst, which demonstrates just how great His grace is. In Romans 6 Paul discussed reasons Christians can no longer think and live in the old ways of sin. Believers have died to the old life by being baptized into Jesus's death and raised into new life through His resurrection. We serve a new Master who liberated us from bondage to sin and empowers us to grow in faith, thus producing the spiritual fruit that shows we have eternal life. Through our obedience, we display Christ and His character to the world. Only by allowing Christ to live in us can we truly have an impact for the kingdom of God.

H

E

A

R

T

DAY 221 | ROMANS 7-8

MEMORY VERSES: ROMANS 8:1; ROMANS 12:1-2

Paul opened chapter 7 by using marriage as an illustration of the meaning of being dead to sin and free from the law's condemning power. Christians are dead to and free from sin, but they belong to Christ. We are set free from the power of the law and can now serve God freely by His Spirit. Still the law has a good purpose in that it makes us aware of our sinfulness and guides us to Christ. Paul concluded the chapter by focusing on the power and presence of Jesus Christ in his life in contrast to his own struggle with sin. In his relationship with Christ, Paul found help. Through Christ we have the Spirit's power in us, enabling us to live in ways that honor God. The Spirit helps us resist sin and provides guidance in making decisions. Furthermore, the Spirit confirms that we are uniquely God's children. We are adopted into God's family and can address God as Father. Because of this, nothing we face here can be compared to the glory that awaits us. Our hope in Christ is certain. Though we often feel discouraged, we have a limitless source of hope. Our challenge is to patiently persevere in the face of any difficulty in the present. Paul closed Romans 8 by affirming God is at work in all things.

H

E

A

R

T

WEEK AT A GLANCE

This week we'll be reading the remainder of Romans. Paul wrote to the Romans about new life in Christ for individuals and for the body of believers. He also emphasized loving one another, which is a relatable instruction for us today.

DAY 222 | ROMANS 9–10

MEMORY VERSES: ROMANS 8:1; ROMANS 12:1-2

THINK ABOUT IT

Reread Romans 10:14-15. Record the progression Paul described for how a person comes to saving faith in Jesus. What is your responsibility if you have a relationship with Jesus?

In Romans 1–8 Paul developed the doctrine of salvation by faith alone. He concluded that God's purposes for His people can never fail. However, it seemed that His purposes for the Israelite people had indeed failed because most of them rejected Jesus as their Messiah. Paul addressed this issue in chapter 9. He emphasized that God is sovereign in all things, including matters of salvation. Next, he explained that God was not being unjust toward those He did not choose by focusing on God's mercy, something that is utterly undeserved and can never be earned. Paul used Pharaoh to illustrate his point of one who did not receive God's mercy. Then Paul emphasized God's patience to Jews and Gentiles alike. The result is that members of both races have access to His mercy and to be saved. For the most part, the Israelites had tried to obtain salvation by obeying God's law, but no humans can ever save themselves, regardless of how zealous they are. No one can do enough good works to earn or receive salvation. Faith—simply believing—and the grace that comes by it are the only way to a right relationship with God.

H

E

MEMORY VERSE

Pick one of the memory verse options for this week—Romans 8:1; Romans 12:1-2—and write the verse.

A

R

T

DAY 223 | ROMANS 11–12

MEMORY VERSES: ROMANS 8:1; ROMANS 12:1-2

God has a great plan for history that includes saving many people—both Jews and Gentiles. At the time when Paul wrote, God's saving purposes centered on many Gentiles coming to faith in God. The day will come when God's saving plan will be accomplished as Jews and Gentiles acknowledge Him as both Lord and Savior. Our response should be praise for the wonder of His saving plan. Romans 12 marks the most important transition in Romans as Paul moves to the "So what?" question. What difference should salvation make in the life of a believer? The first effect of salvation is that we offer our very lives to God in sacrifice and worship by committing to live for Him. We are to seek transformation in how we think through the Word of God, which will result in knowing and experiencing the will of God as well as worshiping God. Our salvation impacts the church body, too, as we use our spiritual gifts wisely to serve others. Paul was aware that it is possible to exercise the gifts of the Spirit without displaying the fruit of the Spirit—specifically love. For that reason, he took some time to remind his readers that Christian love is genuine, opposed to evil, and committed to what is good.

DAILY CHALLENGE
Romans 12:9-21 gives a list of dos and don'ts in the Christian life. Make the list below and see how many you can find in each category.

H

E

A

R

T

DAY 224 | ROMANS 13–14

MEMORY VERSES: ROMANS 8:1; ROMANS 12:1-2

DAILY CHALLENGE

"Love your neighbor as yourself. Love does no wrong to a neighbor. Love, therefore, is the fulfillment of the law."

—Romans 13:9b-10

On a separate piece of paper, write Romans 13:9b-10 and hang it in a prominent spot in your home.

MEMORY VERSE

Continue practicing the memory verse you chose. Write out as much of it as you can from memory, and then check to see how you did.

In Romans 12 Paul dealt with how a follower of Christ is to relate to God and to the church. As he continues to unpack the effects of salvation in a person's life, he provides instruction on how salvation impacts a person's relationship with government and neighbors, whether Christian or not. As far as government is concerned, Christians are expected to show respect for leaders and to pay taxes. Paul reminded his readers that the Ten Commandments teach us how to love one's neighbors. Jesus's disciples are also expected to maintain high moral standards in daily relationships—specifically in sexual behavior, sobriety, and integrity of speech. Paul's words in Romans 14 continue the theme of relationships with others by encouraging us to maintain unity by not judging others for their convictions and not causing others to stumble into sin. God's kingdom is more important than our rights, so we need to let love determine how we act toward one another.

H

E

A

R

T

DAY 225 | ROMANS 15-16

MEMORY VERSES: ROMANS 8:1; ROMANS 12:1-2

Paul closed his letter to the Romans by calling to mind two examples that help us understand the actions and attitudes our salvation should bring forth—the examples of Jesus and of Paul himself. We glorify God by living in harmony with one another and by remembering the life of the Lord Jesus. Christians ought to treat others the same way Jesus treats His people—with compassion, sacrifice, and grace. Paul also voiced his desire for the Romans to be filled with abundant hope through the Holy Spirit. Paul concluded this letter with personal information about his plans to spread the gospel even farther. As he brought his letter to a close, Paul issued a short warning against those who would disrupt the unity of the church, then complimented the Romans once more for their reputation. Fittingly, the final words of his letter are a doxology of praise to God for His greatness and glory.

H

E

A

R

T

WEEK IN REVIEW

Spend some time reflecting on what you have learned this week. Record a truth from each day that you want to remember, or go back and highlight portions of your journal.

DAY 1:

DAY 2:

DAY 3:

DAY 4:

DAY 5:

DAY 226 | ACTS 20–21

MEMORY VERSES: ACTS 20:24; 2 CORINTHIANS 4:7-10

Paul was finishing up his third period of missionary activity. Having spent three years in Ephesus, he departed, evidently shortly after the episode with the silversmiths. Paul traveled through Macedonia, revisiting the churches there, then went on to Corinth in Greece, where he stayed for three months. Acts 20–21 catalogs several stops on this missionary journey. Among the notable things in these chapters are Paul's words of encouragement to the leaders of the church at Ephesus and the repeated warnings he received about the dangers that awaited him in Jerusalem because of his faith. Despite several warnings Paul continued to Jerusalem. At the temple he was attacked by a mob and likely would have been killed if the Romans had not taken him into custody. These two chapters reveal Paul's undivided focus on the advancement of the gospel. Like Paul, when we are fully convinced of who Jesus is and what He has done, we will be obedient to His call and passionate about His priorities.

H

E

A

R

T

WEEK AT A GLANCE

This week we'll be wrapping up the book of Acts. Paul finished his third missionary journey and then headed to Jerusalem where he was taken into Roman custody. The last several chapters record Paul's journey to Rome, where he had multiple opportunities to share the gospel.

DAY 227 | ACTS 22-23

MEMORY VERSES: ACTS 20:24; 2 CORINTHIANS 4:7-10

Chapters 22–23 relate the events surrounding Paul's imprisonment in Jerusalem and his transfer to Caesarea. After he was arrested, Paul addressed the Jewish mob in the temple courtyard—the same mob that moments before sought to kill him. Paul's speech included proof of his Roman citizenship and of his Jewish identity, and also included a description of Jesus's call in Paul's life—a call he was being obedient to follow, even in chains. When the angry crowd abruptly ended Paul's speech, he was taken into the Roman barracks. A Roman centurion was ordered to flog and interrogate Paul to determine the true nature of the Jews' grievances against him. Paul revealed his Roman citizenship to the centurion, who quickly informed his commanding officer. From that point on, the Romans treated Paul much differently. This situation grieved Paul deeply. In the midst of such circumstances, God reminded Paul that He is always at work and that He would empower Paul to preach the gospel in Rome. God's Word and God's work in our lives strengthen us to continue living for Him.

THINK ABOUT IT
How does God's providential love and care for Paul speak to a difficult situation you are facing this week? Spend some time talking to God, praising Him for His love and taking your concerns to Him.

H

E

A

R

T

MEMORY VERSE
Pick one of the memory verse options for this week—Acts 20:24; 2 Corinthians 4:7-10— and write the verse.

DAY 228 | ACTS 24–25

MEMORY VERSES: ACTS 20:24; 2 CORINTHIANS 4:7-10

THINK ABOUT IT

Paul shows us how our own stories are often the best tool for evangelism. Here are some tips for writing your testimony and what to include:

- What defined your life before you met Jesus?
- How did you meet Jesus?
- How are you different now that you have a relationship with Jesus?
- Include a Scripture that God has used in your life.

The governor Felix called for a formal hearing of Paul's case. Although Paul's accusers brought serious charges against him, they were unable to prove his guilt, leading Felix to postpone the trial until a later date. (Felix never reconvened Paul's trial.) He kept Paul under confinement throughout the remaining two years of his term as governor. Once Felix's replacement came along, the Jewish leaders requested that Paul be brought to Jerusalem for trial. Realizing the danger to his life of traveling to Jerusalem, Paul exercised his right as a Roman citizen to appeal to Caesar. Not long after Paul made his appeal to Caesar (25:12), the Jewish king Agrippa arrived in Caesarea. Festus hoped Agrippa would counsel him in what to do with this man who seemed to have broken no Roman laws. Throughout his ministry Paul seized every opportunity to share the gospel with others, and God continually opened doors to make that a reality. Similarly, when we truly grasp the love God demonstrated for us through the death and resurrection of His Son, it compels us to live for Him and to share that joy with others.

H

E

A

R

T

DAY 229 | ACTS 26-27

MEMORY VERSES: ACTS 20:24; 2 CORINTHIANS 4:7-10

Because King Agrippa voiced interest in hearing from Paul, the apostle had the opportunity to defend himself and his gospel ministry before the king. Paul's testimony became the basis for an appeal. He pressed the king to acknowledge Christ as the Savior foretold by the prophets. The king rose to his feet and ended the hearing. As he departed with Festus, the two agreed on Paul's innocence. Paul was then sent to Rome to appear before Caesar. The journey to Rome ordinarily took a couple of months at most, but Paul's party encountered bad weather, delaying the trip six more months. Because of the weather the ship sailed off course from its normal route. When the crew failed to heed Paul's advice, disaster resulted in the form of a massive storm. In the midst of the crew and passengers' despair, Paul predicted that they all would be delivered, which happened just as he said. Paul's life proves time and again that when we are faithful to God's direction, He remains by our side and sees us through. God gives us innumerable promises to help us endure our storms and point others to Christ.

DID YOU KNOW?

Paul was destined for Rome, but the journey God led him on gave him the chance to witness to three different leaders: Felix, Festus, and King Agrippa. The journey is usually as important as the destination.

MEMORY VERSE

Continue practicing the memory verse you chose. Write out as much of it as you can from memory, and then check to see how you did.

H

E

A

R

T

MEMORY VERSES: ACTS 20:24; 2 CORINTHIANS 4:7-10

WEEK IN REVIEW

Spend some time reflecting on what you have learned this week. Record a truth from each day that you want to remember, or go back and highlight portions of your journal.

DAY 1:

DAY 2:

DAY 3:

DAY 4:

DAY 5:

The ship on which Paul was traveling wrecked on the island of Malta, which is south of Sicily. Paul immediately impressed the island's inhabitants when God delivered him unharmed from a viper's bite. This allowed him to carry out a ministry of healing among the islanders. After the winter had passed and the seas were again safe for travel, Paul's party secured passage to Italy. As they completed their journey to Rome on foot, Paul was met by two separate groups of Roman Christians who had come out to greet him. Once in the city, Paul was allowed to live in an apartment rented at his own expense so long as he remained imprisoned under military guard. Luke's story of Paul ends with Paul being under house arrest in Rome for two years as he awaited his hearing before Caesar. During that time, he freely witnessed to all who came to hear him share the gospel. Paul could have easily allowed his circumstances to override his proclamation of the gospel, but instead of throwing in the towel, he continued to proclaim God's love to all who would listen. We should do the same. Christ calls us to make the most of every opportunity to share the gospel with others.

H

E

A

R

T

DAY 231 | COLOSSIANS 1–2

MEMORY VERSES: EPHESIANS 2:8-10; COLOSSIANS 2:6-7

Paul wrote his letter to the Colossians during his imprisonment in Rome. The letter primarily served to correct misunderstandings in the church body by false teachers who were urging believers to blend other religious ideas with Christianity. The theme that dominates the letter is the centrality or superiority of Christ. Paul maintained that Jesus is not only the Creator but also the Sustainer of all things. As such, He is more than able to bring about our reconciliation to God through His cross. Next, Paul transitioned to the main point of his letter in chapter 2 by attacking a false doctrinal teaching that had become a problem for the Christians in Colossae. Paul challenged the believers to continue demonstrating commitment to Christ and gratitude for the privileges that belonged to them in Him. Our lives should be grounded on the supreme foundation of Jesus, and our faith should be fixed on Him as a result. When we see Jesus like this and lose sight of our own lives in His greatness, we finally understand who we truly are and why we were created.

H

E

A

R

T

WEEK AT A GLANCE
This week we'll be reading Colossians and Ephesians. Paul wrote both of these letters from Rome while in prison. Two of the key texts we'll study are Paul's teaching about Christ being supreme and sufficient, and his challenge to put on the armor of God to withstand the schemes of the devil.

DAY 232 | COLOSSIANS 3–4

MEMORY VERSES: EPHESIANS 2:8-10; COLOSSIANS 2:6-7

THINK ABOUT IT

Compare the things Paul says to "put to death" in Colossians 3:5 with the attitudes and behaviors you're to "put on" from 3:12-14. Center your prayer time around asking for the Holy Spirit's power to live in this manner today.

MEMORY VERSE

Pick one of the memory verse options for this week— Ephesians 2:8-10; Colossians 2:6-7— and write the verse.

Colossians 1–2 forms the theological or doctrinal section of Colossians, while chapters 3–4 compose the practical part of Paul's letter. After the apostle had dealt with theological issues facing the Colossians, he proceeded to turn to practical concerns related to their daily lives and their call to pursue holy living. Paul reminded them that, through their conversion experiences, the Colossian believers had died to their old way of life and had risen with Christ to walk in newness of life, as symbolized through baptism. With that reminder, Paul then dealt with some of the most prevalent sins of the first-century Greco-Roman world. He provided a list of these attitudes and behaviors that the Colossians were to "put to death" (Col. 3:5) in their lives. In contrast, Paul also provided a list of virtues that these believers were to "put on" (3:12). If the Colossians were to genuinely serve Christ, they had to conduct their lives in a manner worthy of Him. Even today such qualities should be evident in our lives as a result of a right relationship with Christ. We have been given the responsibility to reflect Christ to the world, which means we are to pursue His holiness in all we say and do.

H

E

A

R

T

DAY 233 | EPHESIANS 1-2

MEMORY VERSES: EPHESIANS 2:8-10; COLOSSIANS 2:6-7

Paul's purpose with the letter to the Ephesians was to communicate God's redemptive plan and power and then to challenge his readers to become everything God wanted them to be as His people. At the start of this letter, Paul describes at length the wonder of God's plan of salvation. Paul revealed that God's plan is much more extensive than simply saving individual people in isolation. God gives of His power to the church to enable believers to live for Him and to carry out His gospel mission in the world. Paul also reminded his readers of how desperate and depraved their condition was before they responded to the gospel. He then declared the power of God's undeserved grace toward them. Finally, he summarized the way in which believers' good works are the result of salvation. Paul then emphasized the corporate or relational dimension of salvation. What matters most about us is not what the world tells us, how people around us see us, or even how we see ourselves. Our identity is determined by what God says about us. Apart from Christ we were dead and hopeless. But in Christ we are alive and will live forever with Him. When we begin believing what God says about us, we can find the freedom to walk in the good works He has planned for us.

DAILY CHALLENGE

Ephesians 2:4-5 includes one of the most powerful statements in all of Scripture: "But God . . . made us alive with Christ." Draw a picture or write a prayer of gratitude to God for the grace He has shown you in saving you from sin and death.

H

E

A

R

T

DAY 234 | EPHESIANS 3-4

MEMORY VERSES: EPHESIANS 2:8-10; COLOSSIANS 2:6-7

DAILY CHALLENGE

After you finish your reading and journaling for today, reflect on these questions:
Of all the broad commands given in Ephesians 4 for Christian living, which command does God seem to be challenging you with most today?

How can you rely on His grace and strength to respond to that challenge?

MEMORY VERSE

Continue practicing the memory verse you chose. Write out as much of it as you can from memory, and then check to see how you did.

In Ephesians 2 Paul had developed his understanding of God's salvation. Here in Ephesians 3 Paul pointedly reminded the readers of his personal role in spreading the good news. Paul's ministry was a gift of grace—an example of accepting opportunities to serve God. Paul's closing prayer highlights God's power, Christ's love, and believers' experience of God's power. As we experience God's strength, we will be equipped to fulfill everything to which God calls His people also. Right thinking about God and salvation will have a practical effect on the way a believer lives today. After reminding them that God had called them to walk worthy, Paul reviewed the matter of spiritual gifts. He then urged the believers to work together for their collective good, using the analogy of a physical body growing to maturity. Paul also contrasted the moral behavior of Christians with the behavior of non-Christians. Simply put, believers are to live differently. We are to be different in our moral behavior, our desires, our speech, our relationships, our priorities, and our very identities.

H

E

A

R

T

DAY 235 | EPHESIANS 5-6

MEMORY VERSES: EPHESIANS 2:8-10; COLOSSIANS 2:6-7

In Ephesians 4 Paul described how Christians are to live uniquely and distinctly, set apart for Christ. Ultimately, we are called to imitate Christ. Because God is love, we are to extend His love toward others. Because God is pure in speech and behavior, we are to behave without impurity. Because God is light, we are to live as children of the light. As Paul continued writing to the Ephesian Christians about how God expects His people to behave, he came to consider family relationships. After all, if one's faith does not measurably make marriages stronger or make for a better relationship between parents and children, it will be difficult to commend others to do the same. Paul closed his letter with a call to be prepared for the spiritual battle that the Christian life inevitably demands. We live prepared by putting on the armor of God, always available to us as His children. No matter what we face, we must rely on the immovable strength and protection of God.

H

E

A

R

T

DAY 236 | PHILIPPIANS 1–2

MEMORY VERSES: PHILIPPIANS 3:7-8; HEBREWS 4:14-16

Paul's letter to the Philippians was deeply personal because he considered them to be gospel partners. They had helped him in the past, and during his imprisonment they had again come to his aid. Paul assured the Philippians of his thankfulness for their partnership with him. He prayed that their love would continue to grow as they discerned the most important things in life and thus be prepared to face God's judgment with confidence. The apostle also wrote that he was convinced his imprisonment was causing the gospel to advance. Paul viewed his circumstances as a part of God's greater plan for the spread of the gospel, but these verses reflect the tension he felt within himself. Paul was not afraid of death, but he felt torn between the desire to depart and be with Christ and the desire to remain in the flesh and help the Philippians grow in the faith. But whatever the outcome, Paul had the assurance that Christ would be glorified and that the gospel would not be defeated. As Paul encouraged his friends to greater unity, he cited the example of Christ to inspire unity and humility. When we imitate Christ, we shine as His light in the world, displaying to others the good news of the gospel.

WEEK AT A GLANCE

This week our reading will be the books of Philippians and Hebrews. Paul wrote to the church at Philippi while he was in prison and thanked them for their partnership in the gospel. Paul learned endurance through his many hardships and still found his joy and hope in Christ. As we read through Hebrews, we'll see many connections between God's promises in the Old Testament and their completion in Christ.

H

E

A

R

T

DAY 237 | PHILIPPIANS 3-4

MEMORY VERSES: PHILIPPIANS 3:7-8; HEBREWS 4:14-16

Philippians 3 deals with Paul's personal experience in Christ. He referred to his background in Judaism and contrasted it with his present life in Christ. Though Paul experienced every privilege Judaism offered, he did not regret his decision to follow Christ. In fact, he considered his past rubbish compared to Christ. Paul described his life in Christ as one of continual striving to reach the goal of maturity in Christ. Further, he exhorted the Philippians to imitate him in their quest for spiritual maturity. In Philippians 4 Paul concluded his message to his friends by challenging, instructing, and thanking them. Though the Philippians had struggles, Paul still loved them and encouraged them to grow in their relationship with Christ and to focus on eternity at all times. Our relationship with Christ involves a growing and personal understanding with Him, which shapes our entire outlook on life. We become spiritually stagnant when we allow our good works to manipulate us into thinking we are not in need of spiritual growth. We also become spiritually sidetracked when we allow past failures to stifle future maturity.

H

E

A

R

T

THINK ABOUT IT
Paul desired to know Christ better, above all else. How does your desire in this area compare to Paul's? Pray specifically for an increased desire in this area of your life today.

MEMORY VERSE
Pick one of the memory verse options for this week—
Philippians 3:7-8;
Hebrews 4:14-16—
and write the verse.

DAY 238 | HEBREWS 1-2

MEMORY VERSES: PHILIPPIANS 3:7-8; HEBREWS 4:14-16

READ ON

Hebrews is full of Old Testament verses and prophecies that describe the person and work of Jesus. Check out this list just from chapter 1:

- Psalm 2:7
- 2 Samuel 7:14
- 1 Chronicles 17:13
- Deuteronomy 32:43
- Psalm 97:7
- Psalm 104:4
- Psalm 45:6-7
- Psalm 102:25-27
- Psalm 110:1

Although the writer of the book of Hebrews is unknown, his purpose is clear: Hebrews was written to content Christians who needed encouragement to grow into mature followers of Christ. Throughout Hebrews the writer emphasized Jesus's superiority to everything the Jews' religious system offered. The writer began by declaring that in the past God had spoken through the prophets, but now, God spoke through His Son, Jesus. In light of Jesus's superiority, the writer warned believers against neglecting the salvation God provided through His Son. God gave humans the assignment of managing His creation. People, however, had not done so. Genesis 3 makes clear that sin had prevented people from fulfilling God's purpose for them. Hebrews 2 shows that Jesus became human to provide a solution to humankind's sin problem. He did for people what they could not do for themselves. Through His death He made salvation available. In this way Jesus is the High Priest who gave Himself for people so they could be forgiven. Only through faith in God can people reach the fulfillment of all that He made them to be.

H

E

A

R

T

DAY 239 | HEBREWS 3-4

MEMORY VERSES: PHILIPPIANS 3:7-8; HEBREWS 4:14-16

In chapter 3 the writer turned to the examples or models of faithfulness that both Jesus and Moses gave. While Moses was a faithful servant among God's people, Jesus is the faithful Son over God's people. Then the writer quoted Psalm 95:7-11 as a warning against the readers being unfaithful to God and rebelling against Him. They were to be wary lest they harden their hearts against God's will. Furthermore, they were not to allow unbelief to cause them to stand off from God and His will for them. Rather, they were to encourage one another daily and to be true to their professions of faith in Christ. In chapter 4 the writer expressed his desire that his readers obey God and enter His rest—the spiritual reality of which the promised land was a symbol. The writer stressed that genuine believers have entered God's rest through faith and obedience. Because God sees us as we are, we must confess and repent of our sins so we can be forgiven. Then we will find true, unshakable rest that transcends the circumstances of life.

THINK ABOUT IT

Read Hebrews 4:12-13 and reflect on how these words have proven true for you during this year-long Bible reading journey you are taking. How has your view of God's Word changed over the course of your year?

MEMORY VERSE

Continue practicing the memory verse you chose. Write out as much of it as you can from memory, and then check to see how you did.

H

E

A

R

T

WEEK IN REVIEW
Spend some time reflecting on what you have learned this week. Record a truth from each day that you want to remember, or go back and highlight portions of your journal.

DAY 1:

DAY 2:

DAY 3:

DAY 4:

DAY 5:

DAY 240 | HEBREWS 5-6

MEMORY VERSES: PHILIPPIANS 3:7-8; HEBREWS 4:14-16

Just as God called the Israelites' high priests to their roles, He also called Jesus to be the ultimate High Priest. Unlike human high priests, however, Jesus was sinless; He did not need to offer sacrifices for Himself. Jesus is qualified, as God's Son who died for people's sins, to be Savior and High Priest for everyone who will trust Him. The writer then turned to the problem of his readers' spiritual immaturity and warned against arrested development. He lamented over the fact that his readers should have been spiritually mature but were not. They needed someone to teach them the basic Christian doctrines. They were still spiritual infants, so his advice was to take deliberate action to grow in their faith, love, and hope. They were not to become lazy but were to imitate worthy examples of faith and perseverance. At the close of chapter 6, we are reminded that God's faithfulness to His promises should encourage believers to maintain their hope in Him and in eternity. Because of Jesus's high priesthood, we have solid hope anchored in what Jesus has done on our behalf.

H

E

A

R

T

DAY 241 | HEBREWS 7

MEMORY VERSES: GALATIANS 2:19-20; 2 CORINTHIANS 5:17

The writer of Hebrews wrapped up chapter 6 by stating that because of Jesus's high priesthood, believers have hope anchored in what Jesus has done on our behalf. In chapter 7 the writer explains how the priesthood of Melchizedek was far superior to Abraham and Aaron's priesthood. The argument made is that if the sacrificial system under Aaron's priestly line could have redeemed people, no need would have existed for a high priest in Melchizedek's order to come. But it couldn't, so Jesus came as High Priest in that order. Jesus is the Son of God and eternal with God Himself, so the hope provided through Jesus's work as High Priest is guaranteed. Because His priesthood is forever, what Jesus did for the salvation of sinners is permanent, and believers' hope is secure.

H

E

A

R

T

WEEK AT A GLANCE
As we finish the book of Hebrews, we'll read about Jesus being our great High Priest and our ultimate sacrifice. Toward the end of the week, we'll read Hebrews 11, which lists many biblical examples of faithfulness. All of these people died before having received what was promised to them. Talk about faith! Let's dive in.

DAY 242 | HEBREWS 8-9

MEMORY VERSES: GALATIANS 2:19-20; 2 CORINTHIANS 5:17

DAILY CHALLENGE

Read Hebrews 9 again, looking for all of the ways the tabernacle and sacrificial system from the Old Testament pointed forward to Jesus. Spend time worshiping God for the hope you have in Jesus. Then consider whom you need to share this hope with this week, and make it a point to do so.

In Hebrews 8–9 the writer continued his emphasis on Jesus as the kind of High Priest believers need by bringing attention to God's Old Testament covenant and the tabernacle under Moses. The writer described Jesus as the Priest of the true tabernacle and the Mediator of a better covenant. From God's original design, the tabernacle and its rituals were symbols that pointed forward to Jesus and the redemption from sins His sacrifice would bring. He offered the perfect, once-and-for-all sacrifice—Himself. This superior sacrifice can cleanse us and make us fit to serve God. To ratify the old covenant, Moses sprinkled the blood of sacrifices on "the tabernacle and all the articles of worship" (Heb. 9:21). To ratify the new covenant, Jesus offered His very blood. With His death, Jesus offers us permanent forgiveness for sins and eternal life in the presence of God.

MEMORY VERSE

Pick one of the memory verse options for this week—Galatians 2:19-20; 2 Corinthians 5:17—and write the verse.

H

E

A

R

T

DAY 243 | HEBREWS 10

MEMORY VERSES: GALATIANS 2:19-20; 2 CORINTHIANS 5:17

The writer of Hebrews was convinced that the Jews' sacrificial system was powerless to cleanse people of their sins. He emphasized the system's inability to make anyone right with God and spiritually mature. The writer turned to the Old Testament to demonstrate that Jesus accomplished what the old covenant's sacrificial system could not. Through Jesus's perfect sacrifice, people of faith are made right with God and are set on a path to spiritual maturity. In verse 19 the author moves from theological to practical teaching as he gives direction on how people live out their faith in Jesus and His sacrifice. Our faith that Jesus is the sinless, eternal High Priest who offered Himself as the perfect, once-for-all-time sacrifice for our sins should be reflected in our behavior. The writer urged them to draw near to God in faith and purity, holding firmly to their confession of hope with the assurance of God's faithfulness. The instructions in Hebrews 10 remind us that the pursuit of God and the acceptance of sin cannot coexist in the life of the Christian.

THINK ABOUT IT

The writer of Hebrews gave three commands that arise out of knowing that Jesus is your great High Priest (10:22-24). What are they? How does knowing that Jesus is your great High Priest enable you to obey these commands?

H

E

A

R

T

DAY 244 | HEBREWS 11

MEMORY VERSES: GALATIANS 2:19-20; 2 CORINTHIANS 5:17

READ ON

The stories of those listed in Hebrews 11 can be found in the following passages:

- Abel – Genesis 4
- Enoch – Genesis 5
- Noah – Genesis 6–9
- Abraham – Genesis 12–25
- Isaac – Genesis 25–28
- Jacob – Genesis 28–36
- Joseph – Genesis 37–50
- Moses – Exodus 3–13
- Israelites at exodus – Exodus 13–14
- Jericho – Joshua 6
- Rahab – Joshua 2

MEMORY VERSE

Continue practicing the memory verse you chose. Write out as much of it as you can from memory, and then check to see how you did.

Often referred to as the hall of faith, Hebrews 11 outlines men and women who displayed exceptional faith in God. First, the writer defines faith in terms of trusting God to the extent of having assurance of His promised blessings. A person cannot please God without faith, so the writer pointed to Noah and Abraham as examples of men who demonstrated faith by their actions. A major aspect of faith is to trust God when we do not experience the fulfillment of all His promises, as Abraham and Sarah modeled. Sometimes we will experience tests of our faith, like Abraham and Moses. Numerous other Old Testament saints demonstrated faith in God. They did not see God's ultimate promise fulfilled, but through their faith God bore witness to its fulfillment. All of these examples show us that genuine faith is demonstrated in our obedience to what God says. Real faith is trusting God with our lives, including our future. God is looking for this kind of faith in His people.

H

E

A

R

T

DAY 245 | HEBREWS 12

MEMORY VERSES: GALATIANS 2:19-20; 2 CORINTHIANS 5:17

In Hebrews 11 the writer described what faith looks like for the Christ follower as modeled by the Old Testament saints. In chapter 12 he likened the life of faith as a marathon that requires great endurance. Along the way we will face difficulties, some of which are discipline from God. We can endure these seasons by growing spiritually through such opportunities. Like an earthly father's discipline, which may be painful but yields positive results, God's chastisement of His children is difficult to receive. However, it's always meant for redemption not condemnation. From this chapter we are also challenged to strive for spiritual health and holiness, and we are encouraged to greater service. When we truly understand the sacrifices God has made to draw us back to Himself, as the writer described earlier in his letter, then we will desire to show Him gratitude, which we do primarily through serving and worshiping Him. Through Christ we are also united to one another in deeper community.

H

E

A

R

T

WEEK IN REVIEW
Spend some time reflecting on what you have learned this week. Record a truth from each day that you want to remember, or go back and highlight portions of your journal.

DAY 1:

DAY 2:

DAY 3:

DAY 4:

DAY 5:

DAY 246 | 1 TIMOTHY 1–3

MEMORY VERSES: 2 TIMOTHY 2:1-2; 2 TIMOTHY 2:15

In addition to the letters Paul wrote to churches, he also wrote letters to individuals whom he discipled to be leaders and pastors. Paul began investing in Timothy's life when he was a teenager. Timothy became a son in the faith to Paul as he accompanied Paul on his missionary journeys. Paul displays humility by reminding him of his own sinfulness and need for Christ's forgiveness. He warns Timothy about false teachers and instructs him on the importance of sound Christian doctrine to combat their heresies. Next, Paul gave Timothy specific instructions about church and worship practices, including prayer, teaching, gender roles, and leadership. All of these reminders prove that our character and actions are important to God, which result in true worship.

H

E

WEEK AT A GLANCE
Believe it or not, you're only three weeks away from finishing this Bible-reading plan! I am so proud of you for making the living and active Word of God a priority in your life this past year. This week we spend time in three more New Testament letters—1 and 2 Timothy and 1 Peter. Let's get started.

A

R

T

DAY 247 | 1 TIMOTHY 4-6

MEMORY VERSES: 2 TIMOTHY 2:1-2; 2 TIMOTHY 2:15

Paul reminded Timothy that he had been put in a position of responsibility to be a good example to other believers. Paul challenged him by offering a series of reminders about what it means to be a Christian role model. An exemplary Christian should extend respect to those in different life stages, compassion to those who need it, and support to leaders of the church. In chapter 6 Paul emphasizes the foolishness of greed and the wise pursuit of godliness. To make this point, Paul contrasted the eternal benefit of godliness and contentment versus the temporal benefit of material wealth. The love of money is a terrible trap, but those whom God has blessed with riches are expected to use it for the good of God's kingdom. These three chapters emphasize the importance of godly living. The pursuit of godliness is an important aspect of the Christian life, and it's how we ensure we're following God and growing in our faith. When we're devoted to our relationship with God and invested in spiritual training, He uses us to make a difference in the world, just as He used Timothy and Paul.

H

E

A

R

T

DAILY CHALLENGE

Spiritual disciplines are practices and habits that help the believer grow in Christlikeness. The most common include:

- Prayer
- Fasting
- Bible study
- Solitude
- Simplicity
- Submission
- Service

Pick one or two disciplines from this list that you want to become a part of your daily life, and ask a friend to join you as you grow in these disciplines.

MEMORY VERSE

Pick one of the memory verse options for this week—2 Timothy 2:1-2; 2 Timothy 2:15—and write the verse.

DAY 248 | 2 TIMOTHY 1-2

MEMORY VERSES: 2 TIMOTHY 2:1-2; 2 TIMOTHY 2:15

THINK ABOUT IT

THINK ABOUT IT

"You, therefore, my son, be strong in the grace that is in Christ Jesus. What you have heard from me in the presence of many witnesses, commit to faithful men who will be able to teach others also."

—2 Timothy 2:1-2

Take these words from Paul and make them your own prayer today. Pray for strength in grace and a committment to discipling others.

It is unknown exactly how much time passed between Paul's first letter to Timothy and the second one, but it is clear that Paul's circumstances had changed drastically. The letter of 2 Timothy is thought to be Paul's last letter, and he wrote it from a prison cell in Rome just prior to his execution. The apostle's sense of urgency is evident throughout this letter. Paul reminded Timothy of the content of the gospel message, which is built on Jesus. Using himself as the model, Paul reminded Timothy that discipleship should be paramount in his ministry. Effectiveness in ministry would be determined by how well he passed on what he heard from Paul. He used several illustrations from those who endure hardship in order to achieve a worthwhile goal: soldiers, athletes, and farmers. The various teachings Paul gave in these two chapters were meant to spur Timothy on toward holy living. Paul's teaching to Timothy helps us see that God calls us to regularly practice repentance both by turning away from sin and actively submitting our lives to Christ.

H

E

A

R

T

DAY 249 | 2 TIMOTHY 3-4

MEMORY VERSES: 2 TIMOTHY 2:1-2; 2 TIMOTHY 2:15

In the second half of 2 Timothy, Paul shifted his focus to the days that lay ahead for Christians, days of persecution and godlessness. Paul identified a number of sinful behaviors that will characterize unbelievers living in the last days. Timothy was to avoid these behaviors and the people practicing them. Instead, Timothy's responsibility was to emphasize God's truth. Paul also warned Timothy of the need to be prepared for persecution and equipped for right living. Timothy's guide—and our guide today—through all these difficulties must be the inspired Word of God, which would profit him in all areas of belief and behavior. Because of the power of God's Word and the prevalence of sin in society, Paul reminded Timothy to preach the Word at all times and in all seasons. To preach includes more than standing behind a pulpit to deliver a sermon. We all have opportunities to make known the truth of God's Word. We must live the faith and be available as witnesses to the truth all the time.

DAILY CHALLENGE
What opportunity might you have this week to proclaim God's Word to someone who needs it?

H

Be on the lookout for any and all opportunities, and pray for the courage and boldness not to pass them up.

E

MEMORY VERSE
Continue practicing the memory verse you chose. Write out as much of it as you can from memory, and then check to see how you did.

A

R

T

WEEK IN REVIEW

Spend some time reflecting on what you have learned this week. Record a truth from each day that you want to remember, or go back and highlight portions of your journal.

DAY 1:

DAY 2:

DAY 3:

DAY 4:

DAY 5:

DAY 250 | 1 PETER 1-2

MEMORY VERSES: 2 TIMOTHY 2:1-2; 2 TIMOTHY 2:15

Included among the books of the New Testament are two letters the apostle Peter wrote to groups of Christians. In his first letter, Peter addressed both Jewish and Gentile Christians who were experiencing violent persecution. Peter wrote to encourage his readers to persevere in their faith and to brace for future attacks. These teachings have implications on our lives as Christ followers today. The basis for Christian hope is Jesus's resurrection and the promise of eternal life. In light of eternity, our trials are temporary and serve to refine our faith. As we await Jesus's return, we are to live holy lives. In obedience to God, we are to seek to reflect His holiness in our behavior, which is possible because we have been redeemed from our old, sinful way of life. In chapter 2 Peter uses several images to help us understand how we have been changed by Christ. We have been given a new diet (spiritual milk that helps us grow in Christlikeness), a new house (the church), and a new family (God's children). God made us such in order that we will tell the world about who He is and what He has done.

H

E

A

R

T

DAY 251 | 1 PETER 3-4

MEMORY VERSES: 1 PETER 2:11; 1 JOHN 4:10-11

After teaching on how Christians are to behave amid persecution, Peter turned his attention to Christian wives and counseled them to submit to their own husbands, to focus on inner purity rather then on outer attire, and to extend goodwill toward others. He challenged the husbands to honor their wives as having an equal status spiritually. Peter also encouraged believers to get along with one another. They were to bless one another through sympathy, compassion, love, and humility. Repeatedly throughout his letter, Peter returned to the topic of suffering. The emphasis in chapter 4 is on sharing in Christ's suffering and resting in the promises that come through His victory over sin and death on the cross. With Christ as our example, we are to foster the same resolve Jesus had in regard to obeying God's will and loving and serving others. Because of the Holy Spirit's active presence in our lives, we are empowered both to endure suffering and to live for Christ.

H

E

A

R

T

WEEK AT A GLANCE
This week we'll be reading in 1 and 2 Peter and 1 John. Peter wrote his letters to the believers who were exiled and scattered throughout the world. We're reminded that as believers we suffer in faith, but we don't lose heart. Our hope is built on Jesus Christ. John reminded his readers of the love of God and challenged them to stand firm in their faith in the face of false teaching.

MEMORY VERSES: 1 PETER 2:11; 1 JOHN 4:10-11

THINK ABOUT IT

"[Cast] all your cares on him, because he cares about you." –1 Peter 5:7

God desires for His children to cast their cares, concerns, and anxieties on Him because He cares about them and will carry them for us. Rest in your relationship with Jesus today.

MEMORY VERSE

Pick one of the memory verse options for this week—1 Peter 2:11; 1 John 4:10-11—and write the verse.

Peter closed his first letter by emphasizing the need for humility in every aspect of our lives, especially in our relationships. Peter warned against the rise of pride in one's life and expected all believers to relate to one another and to God in humility. His exhortation is especially important in light of the presence of the devil, who actively targets Christians even today. Peter concluded his letter by encouraging Christians with the promise that the sovereign God would help them endure any trial that comes their way. While his first letter was meant to encourage believers in the midst of persecution, his second letter was directed to the general body of believers. It primarily emphasizes practical Christian living and growing in the knowledge of God. In chapter 1 Peter described the ideal character of a believer and provided proof for the trustworthiness of the gospel. Believers' lives are to be rooted in their faith in God, which will grow as they practice it and seek God as He has revealed Himself in Jesus Christ. The gospel the apostles preached is a trustworthy source for this knowledge, and it remains as true today as it was when they spoke it.

H

E

A

R

T

DAY 253 | 2 PETER 2-3

MEMORY VERSES: 1 PETER 2:11; 1 JOHN 4:10-11

In chapter 2 Peter explained why it is necessary to base our faith in God on the truth of the gospel: because there are counterfeiters among us. Coming at the church from the outside world was a barrage of heretical and blasphemous teachers and doctrine that had been dressed up to look like Christianity. Peter painted a scathing picture of these teachers. His language is rich with signs and implorations to avoid them at all costs and hold firm to the truth of the gospel that came from those who actually lived with and witnessed the teachings of Jesus. His examination of the false teachers reached a climax in chapter 3, where he reminded his readers to remember what the prophets and apostles of the Lord had spoken. He implored his readers to bear in mind the imminent return of our Lord, who will come like a thief in the night. The expectation of Jesus's return recalls the beginning of the letter, in which Peter implored believers to live upright, moral lives in full devotion to the teachings of Jesus Christ.

DID YOU KNOW?

In Matthew 16:18, Jesus says of His disciple Peter, "You are Peter, and on this rock I will build my church, and the gates of Hades will not overpower it." The record of Peter's ministry from Acts through the letter of 2 Peter shows us that he spent his life pursuing this calling from Jesus.

H

E

A

R

T

DAY 254 | 1 JOHN 1-3

MEMORY VERSES: 1 PETER 2:11; 1 JOHN 4:10-11

DAILY CHALLENGE

How are you challenged in both your love for God and your love for others through today's reading?

Like Peter's first letter, John's first letter is one of assurance and comfort to Christians. He began it with a description of Jesus that emphasized both His humanity and His divinity. Like Peter, John described the life of a follower of Christ, but he used the image of walking in the light to help us understand what the Christian life looks like. He finished the first chapter by encouraging us to reflect the light of our heavenly Father through a morally pure lifestyle. In chapters 2–3 John described a believer's relationship as knowing Jesus personally. We display evidence of a true knowledge of God by obeying His commands, walking as He walked, and loving others as He did. Because of his certainty of Christ's return, John wrote that we must remain in Christ and remember His promise that He will return for us. Our love for others is modeled on Jesus's love for us, which is always sacrificial and costly.

H

E

A

MEMORY VERSE

Continue practicing the memory verse you chose. Write out as much of it as you can from memory, and then check to see how you did.

R

T

DAY 255 | 1 JOHN 4-5

MEMORY VERSES: 1 PETER 2:11; 1 JOHN 4:10-11

Like Peter and Paul, John also addressed the issue of false teachers who were interfering with the spread of the gospel. Because of the very real and dangerous threat false teachings pose to believers' faith, John urged his readers to test all human teachers who claimed to speak with spiritual authority by the Word of God. The mark of genuine faith is the confession that Jesus Christ has come in the flesh. The truth about the nature of Christ is so basic to Christianity that it can never be compromised. Jesus is both fully God and fully man. The false teachers denied that Jesus came in the flesh. John abruptly turned from his discussion of true and false spirits to an appeal for believers to love one another once again. Christians should love one another because God has loved them first. God's supreme demonstration of love is seen in the sending of His Son as a sacrifice for our sins. In chapter 5 John summarized his letter by calling us to lives of obedience, love, and belief—belief in Jesus as the Christ, love for God and for one another, and obedience to God's commands.

H

E

A

R

T

WEEK IN REVIEW

Spend some time reflecting on what you have learned this week. Record a truth from each day that you want to remember, or go back and highlight portions of your journal.

DAY 1:

DAY 2:

DAY 3:

DAY 4:

DAY 5:

DAY 256 | REVELATION 1

MEMORY VERSES: REVELATION 3:19; REVELATION 21:3-4

The Bible begins with a picture of creation, when God gave shape and life to the world and established His relationship with humanity. After sin entered the world, that relationship was broken. The rest of Scripture describes the great lengths God has gone to in order to draw people back to Himself. In the book of Revelation, the final book of the Bible, we get a glimpse of the end days—the time when Jesus will return, God will complete His redemptive work, and those who believe in Him will receive final victory over sin and eternal life with Him. The apostle John, the author of Revelation, began with a vision of Jesus that proves that Jesus is alive, portraying a glory far beyond what we could ever imagine. John's response to this vision of Jesus shows us that Jesus deserves our worship. The more we understand who He is, the better we will understand how to worship Him.

H

E

A

R

T

WEEK AT A GLANCE
You've made it to the last week of *The Bible in a Year!* Can you believe it? What an accomplishment! I pray your love for God and knowledge of Him has grown through your commitment to reading His Word. This week we'll wrap up our reading plan with Revelation, God's future promise to His children.

DAY 257 | REVELATION 2-3

MEMORY VERSES: REVELATION 3:19; REVELATION 21:3-4

Before Jesus showed John a vision of the end times, He gave him messages to send to seven churches located in present-day Turkey. Chapters 2–3 contain those letters. John had been the pastor of the church of Ephesus, one of the seven, and had probably traveled extensively throughout the entire region to visit the people of these churches. His rapport with these churches would have likely made them listen to the words of the letters, even if they were harsh (as they sometimes are). At the center of each of the letters is one central call that is still important to us today: remain true to the risen Christ regardless of your present circumstances. In each of the letters that Jesus dictated to John, it is evident that He knew the people at these churches well. He was intimately familiar with their motivations, their strengths, and their weaknesses. In the same way, Jesus knows us well. When we become aware of God's knowledge of us, we are forced to confront our sins and rejoice in His mercy and grace.

H

E

A

R

T

DAILY CHALLENGE

The letters to the churches in Revelation 2–3 were written to real churches full of real Christians. Review the seven letters. Did one of them resonate with you more than the others at this time in your life? What is the application for your own walk with Jesus?

MEMORY VERSE

Pick one of the memory verse options for this week—Revelation 3:19; Revelation 21:3-4—and write the verse.

DAY 258 | REVELATION 4-5

MEMORY VERSES: REVELATION 3:19; REVELATION 21:3-4

DAILY CHALLENGE

As you read through Revelation 4–5, circle all of the words that describe who God is. Underline all of the words that describe what God does. If you are a visual learner, draw a picture based off of John's description of the throne room of heaven. After you've completed each of these activities, reflect on these two chapters. What have you learned about who God is and the way He's at work?

After receiving the letters to the seven churches, John had a vision with two parts: a setting (chap. 4) and a series of events (chaps. 5–8). According to chapter 4, the setting of this vision is the throne room of heaven, which John described in intricate detail. Each of the characters represented in the vision is vividly portrayed and is shown to be worshiping the One on the throne forever. Rich in allusions to the Old Testament, particularly Ezekiel 1:5-10 and Isaiah 6, the picture of the throne room validated the things John was going to describe next. An accurate portrayal of heaven proves that he was a genuine prophet who spoke with divine authority. In chapter 5 John told us what was going on. The One on the throne was holding a scroll in His right hand, but John wept because nobody was worthy even to look at what it said. His tears did not last long, however, for the Lion of the tribe of Judah, who had the appearance of a slaughtered Passover lamb, proved His worthiness to take the scroll and open it. The entire throne room fell down and worshiped Him just before He was to open the seals one by one.

H

E

A

R

T

DAY 259 | REVELATION 18-19

MEMORY VERSES: REVELATION 3:19; REVELATION 21:3-4

Chapters 18–19 detail John's vision of the fall of Babylon and the defeat of the beast and his armies. Babylon, which is used throughout Revelation to refer to the system of the world that has organized in rebellion against God, is the subject of chapter 18. In language that echoes Jeremiah 50–51, John recorded the song of victory over the beast who rose up against God, sung by an angel whose splendor illuminated the earth. In contrast to this angel's victorious song, the world mourns for its great city that was laid to waste. Chapter 19 continues the celebration begun by the angel, and a vast multitude in heaven rejoiced at God's victory. Our God is a God who avenges injustice. John then witnessed the announcement of a wedding ceremony between the Lamb and His bride. With Jesus's entry to claim victory over Babylon and the beast, John witnessed the final defeat over the beast and his armies. As Christians, we find strength and hope for life by realizing that when Jesus comes again, He will defeat the forces of evil. This truth should also compel us to share the hope we have in Christ with everyone we know so that they can share in the same promise.

H

E

A

R

T

DAY 260 | REVELATION 20-22

MEMORY VERSES: REVELATION 3:19; REVELATION 21:3-4

WEEK IN REVIEW
You did it! Spend some time reflecting on what you've learned this week and this year. Record a truth from each day that you want to remember, or go back and highlight portions of your journal.

DAY 1:

DAY 2:

DAY 3:

DAY 4:

DAY 5:

The last three chapters of Revelation focus on two things: Satan's final push and ultimate defeat and a look ahead to our eternal future with God. In chapter 20 John recounted that Satan will be bound for a time and then will make one last push against God before being thrown into hell forever. Chapter 21 begins with the description of the new heaven, new earth, and new Jerusalem—a holy city. Time and again in Scripture we have seen that both creation and humanity were broken by sin, and here we see that God will once and for all make all things new, just as He promised. John closed his book in chapter 22 with a description of the river of life, which symbolizes the eternal life Jesus makes available for us. Just as the Bible began with a description of Eden, which fell, it ends with this description of a new Eden, which will endure forever because of Jesus's redemptive work. As Jesus wrapped up His vision to John, He issued an urgent call to faith. He desired that all people would come to know Jesus, but a time is coming when unbelievers will have no hope of redemption from their sin and no offer of eternal life with God. Until then God wants to use you to help those around you know Him personally.

H

E

A

R

T

DAY 156 | MATTHEW 3–4

MEMORY VERSES: MATTHEW 5:16; MATTHEW 6:33

HIGHLIGHT the verses that speak to you.

"Then Jesus was led up by the Spirit into the wilderness to be tempted by the devil" (Matt. 4:1).

EXPLAIN what this passage means.

Jesus was baptized and now is entering into a forty-day fast. He will be tempted by the devil during this time.

APPLY what God is saying in these verses to your life.

The Spirit led Jesus into this time of temptation. Satan can do nothing unless God allows it. I have gone through seasons of testing and temptation. The Spirit allowed this time in my life.

RESPOND to what you've read.

Lord, You are so good even in the midst of trying and hard times. You are the only one worthy of any credit for anything in my life.

TRUTH to remember and share.

The Spirit is in full control and sometimes leads a person into a time of testing.

SAMPLE MEMORY VERSE CARD

You, therefore, my son, be strong in the grace that is in Christ Jesus. What you have heard from me in the presence of many witnesses, commit to faithful men who will be able to teach others also.

2 Timothy 2:1-2

SAMPLE PRAYER LOG

DATE ASKED	PRAYER REQUEST	DATE ANSWERED

BIBLE-READING PLAN

WEEK 1
- ❏ Genesis 1–2
- ❏ Genesis 3–4
- ❏ Genesis 6–7
- ❏ Genesis 8–9
- ❏ Job 1–2

MEMORY VERSES
Genesis 1:27
Hebrews 11:7

WEEK 2
- ❏ Job 38–39
- ❏ Job 40–42
- ❏ Genesis 11–12
- ❏ Genesis 15
- ❏ Genesis 16–17

MEMORY VERSES
Hebrews 11:6,8-10

WEEK 3
- ❏ Genesis 18–19
- ❏ Genesis 20–21
- ❏ Genesis 22
- ❏ Genesis 24
- ❏ Genesis 25:19-34; 26

MEMORY VERSES
Romans 4:20-22
Hebrews 11:17-19

WEEK 4
- ❏ Genesis 27–28
- ❏ Genesis 29–30:24
- ❏ Genesis 31–32
- ❏ Genesis 33; 35
- ❏ Genesis 37

MEMORY VERSES
2 Corinthians 10:12
1 John 3:18

WEEK 5
- ❏ Genesis 39–40
- ❏ Genesis 41
- ❏ Genesis 42–43
- ❏ Genesis 44–45
- ❏ Genesis 46–47

MEMORY VERSES
Romans 8:28-30
Ephesians 3:20-21

WEEK 6
- ❏ Genesis 48–49
- ❏ Genesis 50–Exodus 1
- ❏ Exodus 2–3
- ❏ Exodus 4–5
- ❏ Exodus 6–7

MEMORY VERSES
Genesis 50:20
Hebrews 11:24-26

WEEK 7

- ❏ Exodus 8–9
- ❏ Exodus 10–11
- ❏ Exodus 12
- ❏ Exodus 13:17–14
- ❏ Exodus 16–17

MEMORY VERSES
John 1:29
Hebrews 9:22

WEEK 8

- ❏ Exodus 19–20
- ❏ Exodus 24–25
- ❏ Exodus 26–27
- ❏ Exodus 28–29
- ❏ Exodus 30–31

MEMORY VERSES
Exodus 20:1-3
Galatians 5:14

WEEK 9

- ❏ Exodus 32–33
- ❏ Exodus 34–36:1
- ❏ Exodus 40
- ❏ Leviticus 8–9
- ❏ Leviticus 16–17

MEMORY VERSES
Exodus 33:16
Matthew 22:37-39

WEEK 10

- ❏ Leviticus 23
- ❏ Leviticus 26
- ❏ Numbers 11–12
- ❏ Numbers 13–14
- ❏ Numbers 16–17

MEMORY VERSES
Leviticus 26:13
Deuteronomy 31:7-8

WEEK 11

- ❏ Numbers 20; 27:12-23
- ❏ Numbers 34–35
- ❏ Deuteronomy 1–2
- ❏ Deuteronomy 3–4
- ❏ Deuteronomy 6–7

MEMORY VERSES
Deuteronomy 4:7; 6:4-9

WEEK 12

- ❏ Deuteronomy 8–9
- ❏ Deuteronomy 30–31
- ❏ Deuteronomy 32:48-52; 34
- ❏ Joshua 1–2
- ❏ Joshua 3–4

MEMORY VERSES
Joshua 1:8-9
Psalm 1:1-2

WEEK 13

- ❏ Joshua 5:10-15; 6
- ❏ Joshua 7–8
- ❏ Joshua 23–24
- ❏ Judges 2–3
- ❏ Judges 4

MEMORY VERSES

Joshua 24:14-15

Judges 2:12

WEEK 14

- ❏ Judges 6–7
- ❏ Judges 13–14
- ❏ Judges 15–16
- ❏ Ruth 1–2
- ❏ Ruth 3–4

MEMORY VERSES

Psalm 19:14

Galatians 4:4-5

WEEK 15

- ❏ 1 Samuel 1–2
- ❏ 1 Samuel 3; 8
- ❏ 1 Samuel 9–10
- ❏ 1 Samuel 13–14
- ❏ 1 Samuel 15–16

MEMORY VERSES

1 Samuel 15:22; 16:7

WEEK 16

- ❏ 1 Samuel 17–18
- ❏ 1 Samuel 19–20
- ❏ 1 Samuel 21–22
- ❏ Psalm 22; 1 Samuel 24–25:1
- ❏ 1 Samuel 28; 31

MEMORY VERSES

1 Samuel 17:46-47

2 Timothy 4:17a

WEEK 17

- ❏ 2 Samuel 1; 2:1-7
- ❏ 2 Samuel 3:1; 5; Psalm 23
- ❏ 2 Samuel 6–7
- ❏ Psalm 18; 2 Samuel 9
- ❏ 2 Samuel 11–12

MEMORY VERSES

Psalms 23:1-3; 51:10-13

WEEK 18

- ❏ Psalm 51
- ❏ 2 Samuel 24; Psalm 24
- ❏ Psalms 1; 19
- ❏ Psalms 103; 119:1-48
- ❏ Psalm 119:49-128

MEMORY VERSES

Psalms 1:1-6; 119:9-11

WEEK 19

- ❏ Psalms 119:129-176; 139
- ❏ Psalms 148–150
- ❏ 1 Kings 2
- ❏ 1 Kings 3; 6
- ❏ 1 Kings 8; 9:1-9

MEMORY VERSES

Psalms 139:1-3; 139:15-16

WEEK 20

- ❏ Proverbs 1–2
- ❏ Proverbs 3–4
- ❏ Proverbs 16–18
- ❏ Proverbs 31
- ❏ 1 Kings 11–12

MEMORY VERSES

Proverbs 1:7; 3:5-6

WEEK 21

- ❏ 1 Kings 16:29-34; 17
- ❏ 1 Kings 18–19
- ❏ 1 Kings 21–22
- ❏ 2 Kings 2
- ❏ 2 Kings 5; 6:1-23

MEMORY VERSES

Psalms 17:15; 63:1

WEEK 22

- ❏ Jonah 1–2
- ❏ Jonah 3–4
- ❏ Hosea 1–3
- ❏ Amos 1:1; 9
- ❏ Joel 1–3

MEMORY VERSES

Psalm 16:11
John 11:25-26

WEEK 23

- ❏ Isaiah 6; 9
- ❏ Isaiah 44–45
- ❏ Isaiah 52–53
- ❏ Isaiah 65–66
- ❏ Micah 1; 4:6-13; 5

MEMORY VERSES

Isaiah 53:5-6
1 Peter 2:23-24

WEEK 24

- ❏ 2 Kings 17–18
- ❏ 2 Kings 19–21
- ❏ 2 Kings 22–23
- ❏ Jeremiah 1–3:5
- ❏ Jeremiah 25; 29

MEMORY VERSES

Proverbs 29:18
Jeremiah 1:15

WEEK 25

- ❏ Jeremiah 31:31-40; 32–33
- ❏ Jeremiah 52; 2 Kings 24–25
- ❏ Ezekiel 1:1-3; 36:16-38; 37
- ❏ Daniel 1–2
- ❏ Daniel 3–4

MEMORY VERSES
Ezekiel 36:26-27
Daniel 4:35

WEEK 26

- ❏ Daniel 5–6
- ❏ Daniel 9–10; 12
- ❏ Ezra 1–2
- ❏ Ezra 3–4
- ❏ Ezra 5–6

MEMORY VERSES
Daniel 6:26-27; 9:19

WEEK 27

- ❏ Zechariah 1:1-6; 2; 12
- ❏ Ezra 7–8
- ❏ Ezra 9–10
- ❏ Esther 1–2
- ❏ Esther 3–4

MEMORY VERSES
Zephaniah 3:17
1 Peter 3:15

WEEK 28

- ❏ Esther 5–7
- ❏ Esther 8–10
- ❏ Nehemiah 1–2
- ❏ Nehemiah 3–4
- ❏ Nehemiah 5–6

MEMORY VERSES
Deuteronomy 29:29
Psalm 101:3-4

WEEK 29

- ❏ Nehemiah 7–8
- ❏ Nehemiah 9
- ❏ Nehemiah 10
- ❏ Nehemiah 11
- ❏ Nehemiah 12

MEMORY VERSES
Nehemiah 6:9
Nehemiah 9:6

WEEK 30

- ❏ Nehemiah 13
- ❏ Malachi 1
- ❏ Malachi 2
- ❏ Malachi 3
- ❏ Malachi 4

MEMORY VERSES
Psalm 51:17
Colossians 1:19-20

WEEK 31

- ❏ Luke 1
- ❏ Luke 2
- ❏ Matthew 1–2
- ❏ Mark 1
- ❏ John 1

MEMORY VERSES

John 1:1-2,14

WEEK 32

- ❏ Matthew 3–4
- ❏ Matthew 5
- ❏ Matthew 6
- ❏ Matthew 7
- ❏ Matthew 8

MEMORY VERSES

Matthew 5:16; 6:33

WEEK 33

- ❏ Luke 9:10-62
- ❏ Mark 9–10
- ❏ Luke 12
- ❏ John 3–4
- ❏ Luke 14

MEMORY VERSES

Luke 14:26-27,33

WEEK 34

- ❏ John 6
- ❏ Matthew 19:16-30
- ❏ Luke 15–16
- ❏ Luke 17:11-37; 18
- ❏ Mark 10

MEMORY VERSES

Mark 10:45
John 6:37

WEEK 35

- ❏ John 11; Matthew 21:1-13
- ❏ John 13
- ❏ John 14–15
- ❏ John 16
- ❏ Matthew 24:1-31

MEMORY VERSES

John 13:34-35; 15:4-5

WEEK 36

- ❏ Matthew 24:32-51
- ❏ John 17
- ❏ Matthew 26:35–27:31
- ❏ Matthew 27:32-66; Luke 23:26-56
- ❏ John 19

MEMORY VERSES

Luke 23:34
John 17:3

WEEK 37

- ❏ Mark 16
- ❏ Luke 24
- ❏ John 20–21
- ❏ Matthew 28
- ❏ Acts 1

MEMORY VERSES

Matthew 28:18-20
Acts 1:8

WEEK 38

- ❏ Acts 2–3
- ❏ Acts 4–5
- ❏ Acts 6
- ❏ Acts 7
- ❏ Acts 8–9

MEMORY VERSES

Acts 2:42; 4:31

WEEK 39

- ❏ Acts 10–11
- ❏ Acts 12
- ❏ Acts 13–14
- ❏ James 1–2
- ❏ James 3–5

MEMORY VERSES

James 1:2-4; 2:17

WEEK 40

- ❏ Acts 15–16
- ❏ Galatians 1–3
- ❏ Galatians 4–6
- ❏ Acts 17–18:17
- ❏ 1 Thessalonians 1–2

MEMORY VERSES

Acts 17:11,24-25

WEEK 41

- ❏ 1 Thessalonians 3–5
- ❏ 2 Thessalonians 1–3
- ❏ Acts 18:18–19:41
- ❏ 1 Corinthians 1–2
- ❏ 1 Corinthians 3–4

MEMORY VERSES

1 Corinthians 1:18
1 Thessalonians 5:23-24

WEEK 42

- ❏ 1 Corinthians 5–6
- ❏ 1 Corinthians 7
- ❏ 1 Corinthians 8–9
- ❏ 1 Corinthians 10–11
- ❏ 1 Corinthians 12–14

MEMORY VERSES

1 Corinthians 10:13; 13:13

WEEK 43

- [ ] 1 Corinthians 15–16
- [ ] 2 Corinthians 1–2
- [ ] 2 Corinthians 3–4
- [ ] 2 Corinthians 5–6
- [ ] 2 Corinthians 7–8

MEMORY VERSES
Romans 1:16-17
1 Corinthians 15:3-4

WEEK 44

- [ ] 2 Corinthians 9–10
- [ ] 2 Corinthians 11–13
- [ ] Romans 1–2; Acts 20:1-3
- [ ] Romans 3–4
- [ ] Romans 5–6

MEMORY VERSES
Romans 5:1
2 Corinthians 10:4

WEEK 45

- [ ] Romans 7–8
- [ ] Romans 9–10
- [ ] Romans 11–12
- [ ] Romans 13–14
- [ ] Romans 15–16

MEMORY VERSES
Romans 8:1; 12:1-2

WEEK 46

- [ ] Acts 20–21
- [ ] Acts 22–23
- [ ] Acts 24–25
- [ ] Acts 26–27
- [ ] Acts 28

MEMORY VERSES
Acts 20:24
2 Corinthians 4:7-10

WEEK 47

- [ ] Colossians 1–2
- [ ] Colossians 3–4
- [ ] Ephesians 1–2
- [ ] Ephesians 3–4
- [ ] Ephesians 5–6

MEMORY VERSES
Ephesians 2:8-10
Colossians 2:6-7

WEEK 48

- [ ] Philippians 1–2
- [ ] Philippians 3–4
- [ ] Hebrews 1–2
- [ ] Hebrews 3–4
- [ ] Hebrews 5–6

MEMORY VERSES
Philippians 3:7-8
Hebrews 4:14-16

WEEK 49

- ❏ Hebrews 7
- ❏ Hebrews 8–9
- ❏ Hebrews 10
- ❏ Hebrews 11
- ❏ Hebrews 12

MEMORY VERSES
Galatians 2:19-20
2 Corinthians 5:17

WEEK 50

- ❏ 1 Timothy 1–3
- ❏ 1 Timothy 4–6
- ❏ 2 Timothy 1–2
- ❏ 2 Timothy 3–4
- ❏ 1 Peter 1–2

MEMORY VERSES
2 Timothy 2:1-2,15

WEEK 51

- ❏ 1 Peter 3–4
- ❏ 1 Peter 5; 2 Peter 1
- ❏ 2 Peter 2–3
- ❏ 1 John 1–3
- ❏ 1 John 4–5

MEMORY VERSES
1 Peter 2:11
1 John 4:10-11

WEEK 52

- ❏ Revelation 1
- ❏ Revelation 2–3
- ❏ Revelation 4–5
- ❏ Revelation 18–19
- ❏ Revelation 20–22

MEMORY VERSES
Revelation 3:19; 21:3-4

1. *The ESV Study Bible* (Wheaton, IL: Crossway Bibles, 2008).

2. Gerard Van Groningen, "Israel," *Baker's Evangelical Dictionary of Biblical Theology* (Grand Rapids: Baker Books, 1996). Accessed 2 January 2022. Available online at www.biblestudytools.com.

3. Ibid., *The ESV Study Bible.*

4. *Rose Book of Bible Charts, Maps and Time Lines* (Torrance, CA: Rose Publishing, 2005).

5. Ibid.

6. *CSB Disciple's Study Bible* (Nashville, TN: Holman Bible Publishers, 2017).

7. Iva G. May, *W3: Women, Worldview, and the Word,* Chronological Bible Teaching (Germantown, TN: 2007).

8. "Jonathan (Son of Saul)," Logos Factbook. Accessed 4 January 2022. Available online at www.logos.com.

9. "2 Samuel 24:25," *The ESV Study Bible,* 550; "2 Samuel," William MacDonald, *Believer's Bible Commentary* (Nashville, TN: Thomas Nelson, 1995).

10. "Book of First Kings," Logos Factbook. Accessed 4 January 2022. Available online at www.logos.com.

11. "Ezra," Strong's H5830. Accessed online at www.blueletterbible.org.

12. Adapted from "Esther," *NIV Life Application Study Bible* (Colorado Springs, CO: Zondervan), 821.

13. "Faith," Oxford Lexico. Accessed 5 January 2022. Available online at www.lexico.com/en/definition/faith.

14. Andrew Murray, *The True Vine* (Moody Publishers, 2007), 63.

15. Thomas Constable, "Commentary on Matthew 27:55," *Dr. Constable's Expository Notes.* Accessed 2 January 2022. Available online at www.studylight.org/commentaries/dcc/matthew-27.html.

16. Fred L. Fisher, "Stephen," *Holman Bible Dictionary* (Nashville, TN: Holman Bible Publishers, 1991), 1303.

17. C. S. Lewis, *Letters to Malcolm: Chiefly on Prayer* (Harcourt, Brace, and World: 1963), 55-56.

Now you can read through all of the key, foundational passages of the Bible in one year, while still having the flexibility of reading five days per week. And options exist for students and kids too. Each resource uses the HEAR journaling method, allowing for practical application throughout the year-long plans.

Learn more at lifeway.com/foundations

Lifeway

CAMEL
CLOTH-OVER-BOARD

BUTTERSCOTCH
GENUINE LEATHER

GRAY/MINT
LEATHERTOUCH

MARIGOLD
LEATHERTOUCH

Every Christian woman is called to live confidently in her identity—known, free, and loved in Christ. Designed to assist women of any age as they study God's Word, the *CSB Lifeway Women's Bible* will inspire you to laugh, grow, and worship alongside your community.

Available now at CSBLifewayWomensBible.com

CHRISTIAN
STANDARD
BIBLE®